LE BALET COMIQUE DE LA ROYNE

1581

MUSICOLOGICAL STUDIES AND DOCUMENTS

ARMEN CARAPETYAN, Ph. D.
General Editor

LE BALET COMIQUE DE LA ROYNE 1581

Carol & Lander MacClintock

MUSICOLOGICAL STUDIES AND DOCUMENTS

25

LE BALET COMIQUE DE LA ROYNE

1581

Translated by

CAROL AND LANDER MACCLINTOCK

The music transcribed by

Carol MacClintock

1971

AMERICAN INSTITUTE OF MUSICOLOGY

CONTENTS

ILLUSTRATIONS

INTRODUCTION

October 15, 1581 is a significant date in the history of Western music because it marked the production in Paris of the *Balet comique de la Royne*, "the first genuine ballet de cour" and an important step in the development of opera. It is the first known work to intentionally combine dance, poetry, and music in a coherent dramatic whole.

This artistic event must be seen in its proper perspective, against the contemporary artistic, political, and social background. From the artistic and literary standpoint, by 1581 the Italian-inspired Renaissance had almost run its course; the great palaces in the Loire valley had all been built; the great masters of painting were turning more and more to expressive mannerism and the Baroque. In literature the members of the *Pléiade* were still alive and active, notably Ronsard, now an old man, and the protestant D'Aubigné, Antoine de Baïf, Pontus de Tyard and Antoine Jodelle. Their ideas, often derived from the Italians, were most influential in the literary and philosophical circles, especially their attempt to revive classical forms and techniques in the arts.[1] In 1581 the kingdom of France politically and economically was on the brink of chaos. The many years of recurring internecine warfare between the Protestants and the Catholics, culminating in the brutal St. Bartholomew's Massacre in 1572, had disrupted society and reduced the country to penury. The Protestant workmen, the wealth producers, had been driven into exile, so commerce and industry were greatly reduced. Then, too, the extravagance of the court under a succession of Valois kings was a prime factor in the economic *débâcle*. In 1581 the ruler was the incompetent Henry III, who was dominated by that strong-minded and not-too-subtle Florentine, his mother Catherine de' Medici.

This same year of 1581 saw a brief respite in the active fighting in France, and on the occasion of a state marriage the King, possibly at the suggestion of his mother, as Frances Yates guesses,[2] conceived

[1] Frances A. Yates, *The French Academies of the Sixteenth Century*, London, The Warburg Institute, University of London, 1947. 132 *et passim*. I have relied heavily on this work in my discussion.
[2] Yates, *op. cit.*, 258.

the idea of showing to the world the magnificence of which France was capable and at the same time proving that she was solvent. As a matter of fact, it did just the opposite, since the millions of francs spent on the *Balet comique* and other *fêtes* pushed the house of Valois even deeper in debt.

Henry's display of magnificence took the form of a series of elaborate entertainments celebrating the marriage of the Duc de Joyeuse, the King's favorite, to Mlle. de Vaudemont, the Queen's half-sister.[3] The marriage took place on September twenty-fourth and was followed by two weeks of *fêtes* provided by the King and members of the court. The eighth of these "magnificences" was the *Balet comique*, presented on Sunday, October 15, and the celebration finally came to a close with an entertainment given by the Queen Mother on October 22. The only one of these events that has survived is the *Balet comique de la Royne* because the impresario of this production, Baltasar de Beaujoyeux, was so proud of his creation, which he rightly considered unique, that he wrote a complete description of it. In his Preface he makes clear that the intention was not only to present a spectacle of high artistic merit but also to demonstrate by means of allegory and allusion how sound, how firmly grounded was the kingdom of France, and how just and benign the rule of Henry III. However, the immediate reason for the creation of this work was that Queen Louise wished to make a significant contribution to the festivities and to honor them by taking part personally. With this in mind she called in Baltasar de Beaujoyeux and asked him to suggest a *divertissement* which would serve her purpose.

Who was Beaujoyeux? He was an Italian who came to France about 1555 as a member of the Maréchal de Brissac's band of violins and frenchified his Italian name of Baldassare da Belgioioso to Baltasar de Beaujoyeux soon after his arrival. He is said to have been a very competent violinist and a person of wit and ingenuity

[3] The program planned for the "magnificences" exists in a manuscript in the Bibliothèque Nationale. It not only lists the various events but also describes the costumes and accoutrements of the noble participants and indicates to a certain extent the music that was to be performed. See Yates, "Poésie et musique au mariage du Duc de Joyeuse, Paris, 1581", in *Musique et Poésie au XVIe siècle*, Paris, Centre Nationale de la Recherche Scientifique, 1954, p. 241ff.

who had qualities as a courtier which brought him favors from members of the court. "... C'était l'Italien tel que le montrent les traditions florentines, cauteleux, flatteur, industrieux, sachant bien faire marcher de front les intérêts de l'art et ceux de sa bourse."[4] In 1567 he became valet de chambre to Catherine de' Medici and, later, in the same capacity served Henry III, Marie Stuart, Charles IX, and the Duc d'Alençon. When he died in 1587 he was again in Catherine's service and had been made *Écuyer* and *seigneur des Landes*.[5] He had very likely become indispensable in the social and artistic life of the court as a kind of "master of the revels", and undoubtedly it was for this reason that Queen Louise turned to him.

Because time was so short, as he says, Beaujoyeux called in other talent to help him. He himself was impresario, stage manager, and perhaps choreographer, but he turned to Lambert de Beaulieu for the music,[6] and Jacques Salmon, *maître de la musique de la chambre du Roi*, for the performance of it. The Sieur de la Chesnaye, the King's poet and almoner, wrote the text,[7] and Jacques Patin, the King's painter, provided the scenery and possibly also designed the costumes.[8] These were not France's best talent, not in a class with the poet Ronsard and the composer Claude Le Jeune, who had, however, contributed their share to the "magnificences".[9] The performers,

[4] Ludovic Celler, *Les Origines de l'opéra et Le Ballet de la Reine*, Paris, 1868, 136. Brantôme speaks of being honored to be his friend and says Beaujoyeux "estoit de fort gentil esprit et scavoit beaucoup et surtout de fort belles histoires et beaux contes." He also calls him "le meilleur violon de la chrestienté". (*Oeuvres complètes*, ed. Lalanne, IX, 669.)

[5] Henry Prunières, *Le Ballet de cour en France*, Paris, 1914, 78.

[6] Lambert de Beaulieu, a talented singer and gentleman of the court, was one of the musicians closely associated with Thibaut de Courville's and Baïf's *Académie de Poésie et de Musique*.

[7] D. P. Walker suggests that even though the Sieur de la Chesnaye, Beaulieu and Salmon are the only persons named as having composed the text and music, it is quite possible that Baïf and Claude Le Jeune had some part in its preparation. Baïf hoped to extend his movement to drama and was particularly interested in a *ballet mesuré*. ("The influence of *musique mesureé à l'antique*", *Musica Disciplina* I (1946), 146.) This is, however, speculation.

[8] It was quite usual for a court painter to provide scenery and costumes for court theatricals. *Vide* the accounts of Giulio Romano's costumes for a *moresca* in 1542 and Curzio Ardizio's scenery for the *intermedii* for *Gli ingiusti sdegni* of 1583 at Mantua, in C. MacClintock, *Giaches de Wert: Life and Works*, American Institute of Musicology, 1966, pp. 165, 174.

[9] See Yates, *Academies*... p. 271.

as was usual in the sixteenth century, were chosen from talented members of the court and from the King's musicians.

The theme for the Queen's Ballet was the Circe story adapted from Homer. Circe, whose garden according to this plot is somewhere in France, is the evil spirit who dominates men through their baser instincts. She is defeated and subjugated by the virtuous King Henry III with the aid of heaven, personified in Minerva and Jupiter. To the sixteenth century the allegory was clear: the two divinities Jupiter and Minerva symbolized the King and Queen, and their victory over Circe was the victory of the royal party whose laws were driving out vice and war. The Circe legend, then, provided a timely symbolic representation of the state and power of France, and also permitted allegorical interpretations on several levels — moral, political, natural philosophical — suitable to the humanistic atmosphere of the court. At the same time it lent itself to the most splendid kind of artistic production.

Beaujoyeux implies that the idea of the plot was his alone, but it is more likely that the original plan was devised by Agrippa d'Aubigné some five or six years earlier, and that Beaujoyeux, perhaps at the instigation of the King or of Catherine, simply took it over, making some alterations.[10] Since preparations for all the other festivities were well under way when the Queen decided to offer her entertainment, it would seem likely that a plan of some sort must have been ready to hand, and it may well have been D'Aubigné's project that had never been performed.

As an artistic form the *Balet comique* was not without its antece-

[10] D'Aubigné, the Huguenot writer in the entourage of Henri de Navarre and imprisoned with him during the years 1572-1576, states that he was the inventor of the *Ballet comique*. "Ces deux princes [Guise and Navarre] couchoyent, mangeoyent & faisoyent ensemble leurs mascarades, balets et carousels, desquels Aubigné seul estoit l'inventeur, & dès ce temps il dressa le project de la *Circe* que la royne mère ne voulut pas executer, pour la despence; & depuis le Roy Henri troisième l'executa aux nopces du Duc de Joyeuse." (*Oeuvres complètes*, ed. E. Réaume et F. Caussade, Paris, 1873-92. I, 23). Cited in Yates, *Academies*... p. 257. According to Yates, Henry, remembering what he had heard some years earlier about D'Aubigné's Circe ballet, decided to perform it for the celebration of the Duc de Joyeuse's marriage and sent to Gascony (where D'Aubigné was in quasi-exile) "to persons he did not love at all" for the ballet. This may mean that he sent for both D'Aubigné and his ballet or for the ballet alone. (See Yates, *op. cit.* 157-8 for discussion of this point.)

dents. According to Prunières, the *Balet comique* is an outgrowth of a combination of earlier forms, the *mascarade*, Italian *intermedio*, and the more recently popular Italian *pastoral.* Italian forms of entertainment had been introduced into France during the reigns of Louis XII, Charles VII, and Francis I, brought back by the gentlemen of the court who had participated in the various expeditions to Naples and Milan under those monarchs. Italian influence became very strong under Francis I and Catherine de' Medici, when great numbers of Italian artists and musicians were imported for their court. Thenceforth, despite the difficult times of civil war and internal strife, entertainments such as intermedii, ballets, carousels, tourneys and mascarades were favorite divertissements, presented on all major and many less important occasions.

The French were always acutely aware of what was going on in Italy. Letters and reports of ambassadors brought news of court activities across the Alps; the literary men of France, particularly the poets, carried on a constant correspondence with Italian writers, and numerous Italian literary men such as Corbinelli and Del Bene were at the French court. The great Italian poet Tasso visited Paris in 1571 in the *cortège* of Cardinal Luigi d'Este, and Antoine de Baïf and others of the *Pléiade* traveled in Italy. The entertainments of the French court became perhaps even more italianized under Henry III, for he had personally experienced the lavish spectacles provided in his honor in Venice, Ferrara, Mantua, and Turin on his return journey from Poland in 1574.[11] During his reign the famous Italian troupe of comedians who had performed for Henry in Venice, *I Gelosi*, visited Paris in 1575 and there presented the latest theatrical pieces from Italy, perhaps including Tasso's *pastoral*, the *Aminta*, of 1573.

Of all these influences, the *intermedio* was perhaps the most important in the creation of the *Balet comique de la Royne*. The Italian *intermedio*, a single scene with music, elaborate costumes, scenery, and machines, and a minimum of action designed to be performed between the acts of a play, had been adopted and adapted to French

[11] See P. Nolhac et A. Solerti, *Il Viaggio di Enrico III re di Francia e le feste a Venezia, Ferrara e Torino.* 1890.

taste early in the century and was the source for many elements that would later be incorporated in the *ballet de cour*.[12] Entertainments such as the famous *fêtes* of 1539 and 1565 for the marriages of Cosimo de' Medici and of Francesco de' Medici are typical of the lavish *intermedii* that were usual in Florence and other centers on state occasions.[13] As in Italy, so in France. The *Fêtes de Fontainebleau* of 1564, the *Paradis d'amour*, on the occasion of the wedding of Henri de Navarre and Marguerite de Valois in 1572, and the celebrated *Ballet des Polonais*, given in honor of the Polish ambassadors in 1573, matched the Italian *intermedii* in every respect. The French versions cited are similar in tone and technique to the *Balet comique de la Royne* and may be described as direct forerunners. All combine music, poetry, dance, in a unified scene but without dramatic action.[14]

As important and pervasive as the influence of Italy was that of the powerful humanistic trend exemplified in the theories and practice of the members of the *Académie de Poésie et de Musique*. This famous body was founded in 1570 by Jean-Antoine de Baïf, a poet and musician, and Joachim Thibaut de Courville, a *joueur de lyre* and singer in the service of the king, at that time Charles IX. This academy included in its members both *professionels* and *auditeurs*, and its aim was the establishment of a closer union between the arts than had hitherto existed. Many of the outstanding literary men were connected with it — Ronsard, Dorat, Jodelle, Tyard, Mellin de

[12] Prunières says, "Il est indispensable de tenir compte de l'influence des Intermedii italiens en étudiant la création du ballet dramatique français. Nous avon déjà parlé de ces danses figurées, de ces pantomimes, de ces récits chantés, de ces choeurs qui s'intercalaient entre les actes des pièces, tragiques ou comiques, représentées sur les scènes d'Italie, et pénétraient parfois jusqu'au coeur de l'action. À mesure que le théâtre de cour développait dans la Péninsule, cette mode devenait envahissante. En même temps le genre pastoral, qui avait fait ses premiers pas avec l'*Orfeo* de Politian et le *Cefalo* de Nicolò da Correggio, trouvait son expression la plus haute dans l'*Aminte* de Torquato Tasso." (*Op. cit.*, p. 79.)

[13] The music as well as the text of the 1539 *fêtes* survive and show very clearly that their function was solely that of filling in the time between acts, for they have no connection with the action of the comedy nor with each other. Both text and music have been printed in translation and transcription: *A Renaissance Entertainment*: *Festivities for the marriage of Cosimo I, Duke of Florence in 1539*. An Edition of the Music, Poetry, Comedy, and Descriptive Account with Commentary by Andrew C. Minor and Bonner Mitchell. (Columbia, Mo., University of Missouri Press, 1968.)

[14] Prunières, *op. cit.*, 55-57; also Yates, *Academies*... 250.

St. Gelais; and numbered among the musicians were Jacques Mauduit, Eustache du Caurroy, Fabrice Caietan, and Claude Le Jeune, the most talented of them all. Chief among their tenets was the principle that poetry was to be sung or recited to music in the manner of the ancient Greeks, to represent "la parole en chant accomply de son harmonie et melodie, qui consistent au choix, regle des voix, sons et accords bien accomodez pour faire l'effet selon que le sens de la lettre requiert."[15] To this end Baïf and his group created a kind of verse based on Latin quantities, which they called *vers mesurés à l'antique*. They also discussed philosophical and artistic problems in their sessions and were much interested, like the *Pléiade*, in the development and enrichment of the language.[16] The meetings were held in Baïf's house and were often attended by Charles IX, later by Henry III and the Duc de Joyeuse. Its concerts, in which both French and Italian music was performed, were famous. This academy, the precursor of the Florentine *camerata*,[17] did not survive after 1584.

In staging the *Balet* Beaujoyeux, who had for some time been associated with various members of Baïf's *Académie* and was certainly familiar with its principles, consciously attempted to create a work in which the humanistic ideal of the fusion of the arts would prevail. He drew on the old tradition of the tragedy with *intermedii* between the acts, added the ballet, choruses in the (supposedly) ancient style, solo songs accompanied by instruments, placing them all within the

15 From Baïf's and Thibaut's petition addressed to Charles IX for the establishment of this *Académie*. Yates, *Academies*..., App. I.

16 This academy, with its interest in the French language, was the precursor of what later became the *Académie française*, still in existence.

17 The close connection between the Bardi group and the *Académie* is evident from the fact that Rinuccini was in Paris in 1581 and was present at the performance of the *Balet comique*. He undoubtedly brought back a report of it to Florence, for he was impressed by what he saw and heard, since it was in line with the Florentine experiments he had stimulated. He then thought of transplanting to Italy such a dramatico-musical work, but of substituting for recited poetic passages the *recitativo accompagnato*. (See F. Liuzzi, *I Musicisti in Francia*, Rome 1946, p. 125). There were many reciprocal French and Italian influences in the arts during this period and certain known personal connections. Baïf, whose mother was Italian, was often in Italy and fully conversant with Italian letters and music. On the other hand, Italian letterati were frequently in Paris and aware of artistic currents there.

normal theatrical framework of scenery, costumes, machines, and all the other theatrical trappings. In the *Balet comique de la Royne* all the elements are present that were always present in the mascarades, the tourneys, balletti, and other divertissements, but its plan is entirely new, for there is a clear dramatic intention in its construction.

The resultant work is not a true ballet nor is it comical. It is a production where dancing, declamation, solo and choral singing and instrumental music play important and essential, if not equal, parts in the unfolding of a dramatic situation. Beaujoyeux makes this clear in his account of the event. He also explains that he calls it "comique" only because it has a peaceful and happy ending, not because there is anything humorous or funny about it. Perhaps a better designation would have been "comédie ballet", a term often used by Molière a hundred years later.

It is beside the point whether or not Beaujoyeux was the actual inventor of this new type of entertainment. Most likely he had some help from several members of the *Académie* who would have been interested in the creation of such a work of art. The important thing is, that in the *Balet* we can clearly see just how all the arts were indeed combined to create a spectacle which was undoubtedly a great novelty. The truly new feature in this work is that the *intermedio* functions as part of the action, not merely as a diversion between scenes or acts, and provides continuity. In each of the several *intermedii* — the Sirens, the Fountain with its accompanying Tritons, the Satyrs, the Dryads, and the Virtues — after the personages have come in on their *chars* (or on foot) and have sung their songs or dialogues which identify them and link them with the story, they descend from their vehicles or join a group and become part of the continuing action. Even the ballet portions are incorporated in and continue the unfolding plot. The god Mercury comes down from the celestial realms in a cloud, as does Jupiter; both sing stanzas which announce their purpose, then they, too, enter the drama. All the other characters — Opis the nymph, Pan, Minerva — are introduced in similar fashion. The Water Nymphs perform in the first ballet geometrical figures which are supposedly symbolic of the themes of the story and at the end, at the sound of the *clochette*, Circe appears and changes them into statues. The final ballet, again a series of elaborate geometrical figures, was intended as an artistic expression and reinforcement of "the Pythagorean-Platonic core of the Academy — that all things are related to number, both in the outer world of nature and in the inner world of man's soul...",[18] a fitting conclusion to a work that purported to demonstrate so amply the harmony and perfection that reigned in France.

Staging and Scenery

The performance took place in the great *Salle* of the Hotel de Bourbon, not on a stage. The spectators sat at one end, on risers, and in galleries around the sides. The stage decor was distributed around the hall; Circe's palace and garden at one end; on one side, about halfway down the room was Pan's grotto, which concealed a regal organ, and beside it, Pan's wood; on the opposite side was the "golden vault" where the musicians were stationed. The setting remained in place throughout the entire ballet; there were no changes of scene.

Prunières points out that the staging of the *Balet comique* was in no way different from the usual practice employed in previous ballets. The various scenic items of the production were not entirely new, but their combination was; e.g., the silver cloud in which Jupiter and Mercury descended had been used in several previous productions, and the ambulant Fountain greatly resembled the ambulant *Rocher* on which the nymphs in the *Ballet des Polonais* made their entrance. Nevertheless, there were a few novelties. Circe's castle, which was painted and erected on a framework in front of a backdrop in perspective, had hung before it at the beginning of the action a heavy veil or netting which was dropped at the proper moment to reveal Circe's gardens. Installed in the gateway of the castle, in a shell-shaped opening, were numerous small panes of colored glass behind which candles were burning. These cast a kaleidoscopic effect on the scene. Pan's bosky dell was also concealed

[18] Yates, *Academies...*, 248.

by a curtain until the second act, when the Dryads arrived to be seated within it together with Pan.

The machines or floats must have been painted. Despite Beaujoyeux' descriptions which would seem to imply solid structures, it would have been impossible to create the Fountain, for example, out of solid material. There was most likely a framework mounted on a flat truck which could be pulled by several men (or horses), and over this was attached painted cloth. The "burnished gold" and silver reliefs would have been painted in *trompe l'oeil*, and the jet of water imitated by strands of tinsel. In the rather dim flickering candle light which illuminated the hall, the effect would have been quite real. The same may be said of the Sirens' and Tritons' floats. The glittering tails of these marine monsters and the waves surrounding them were painted on cloth.

The "golden vault", opposite Pan's grotto, was said to have been nine by eighteen feet and to have had within it forty musicians. It would have been impossible to place forty performers in such a small space unless, of course, the part which showed in the hall, covered with golden clouds, was simply an extension of a deep recess which extended back under the galleries.

All the scenery and apparatus used were exactly of the kind which had been in use in the court entertainments in Italy and France throughout the sixteenth century and therefore not novelties except in their splendid effect.

The music

The music, performed by voices and instruments, is an important and significant feature of the *Balet comique*. Here, well before the appearance of Florentine monody, are a number of solo songs, unquestionably in the new monodic style: the dialogue of Glaucus and Thetis, Mercury's song, Jupiter's song, and also the song of the four Virtues, in which each one sings a stanza alone as well as one in unison. This is not like Florentine monody, which aimed at recitation in the manner of the Greeks, as they thought; rather it is lyrical solo song, complete with vocal embellishments, and was sung by virtuoso singers of the court — the Sieur de Savornin of the King's music, the Sieur de Beaulieu, and Estienne Le Roy, Abbé de St. Laurent, a famous castrato.

Apart from the *intermedii* of the Tritons, Satyrs, Virtues, and Pan, in which certain accompanying instruments are specified, Beaujoyeux never states exactly which instruments were employed in the various ensembles. He does mention the violins in connection with the dances, but does this mean that only violins were used? He makes it clear that forty musicians were participating, composed of voices and instruments, but again he does not give the proportions of voices to instruments nor the distribution of instruments. One can only speculate that the "orchestra" was composed of the conventional instruments of the period, including flutes, krummhorns, viols, lutes, cornetti, sackbuts, drums, and cembalo.[19]

The remainder of the music was of two kinds: the instrumental pieces for the dances, written for five parts in ordinary mensural music, and the choral music, which was of the kind called *musique mesurée*. This latter, associated exclusively with Baïf's Academy, was the result of an attempt on the part of Baïf and his *confrères* to reproduce, in French, classical prosody based on quantity — *vers mesurés à l'antique*, or metered verse in the ancient manner — sung to music whose rhythms would correspond exactly to those of the poetry.

Of theoretical interest to the poets, in practice it was an impossibility, for the French language, even in the sixteenth century, was based on stress and not on quantity. In his endeavors to ascertain long and short feet in French, Baïf assumed that stressed syllables should be counted as longs, and unstressed syllables as shorts, thus confusing accent and quantity. He established certain rules as to which syllables were always long, but by following these rules he was often led to make an unaccented syllable long and thus cause misplaced stress.[20] This, of course, makes it impossible to read French poetry aloud emphasizing the meter, and if the meter is

[19] In this connection see R. Weaver, "Sixteenth Century Instruments", *Musical Quarterly* XLVII (1961); also L. Celler, *op. cit.*, 237.

[20] See H. Expert, "À propos de la musique française à l'époque de la Renaissance", in *Encyclopédie de la musique*, ed. Lavignac, Paris, 1921, pt. I, v. III, 1261 ff; P.-M. Masson, "Le mouvement humaniste", *op. cit.*, pt. I, v. III, 1299; M. Augé-Chiquet, *La vie, les idées et l'oeuvre* de *de Jean-Antoine de Baïf*, Paris, 1909.

not emphasized it merely sounds much like ordinary French verse. The important thing is, that *vers mesurés* were intended to be *sung* and not read, and in this way a special relationship *was* created between words and music. The principle was that long feet were matched by long note values, short feet by short note values — thus presumably wedding exactly verse and music.

In general the composers wrote the long as exactly equal to two shorts, but it was allowable to use several notes of lesser values for one syllable so long as their total equalled the value of the long note they replaced.[21] However, certain theorists said that any short values might be used, provided the shorts remained shorter than the longs, and this would indeed seem to have been used in practice, for in the 24eme *Livre d'Airs et Chansons* of 1583 the rule of two shorts exactly equalling a long is not followed. In speaking of this print D. P. Walker writes, "The only rhythmic principle with regard to the metre of the text, that all these obey is that a long shall always be longer than a short; the proportion may vary to any extent."[22] Further in the same article he says that it "seems probable, but not certain," that they did not believe that "classical meters had an ictus or plausus in the sense of a regular beat",[23] thus permitting them to adopt a somewhat less rigid rhythm for their *vers mesurés*. This second approach lends more flexibility to the music than strict adherence to the principle of a long always equalling two shorts. The following examples will make this clear.[24]

Long = 2 shorts (Jacques Mauduit)

— ◡ ◡ — ◡ — ◡ — ◡ — ◡ — — — ◡ —

Vous me tu - ez si dou - ce - ment a - vec - que tour-mens tant be - nins

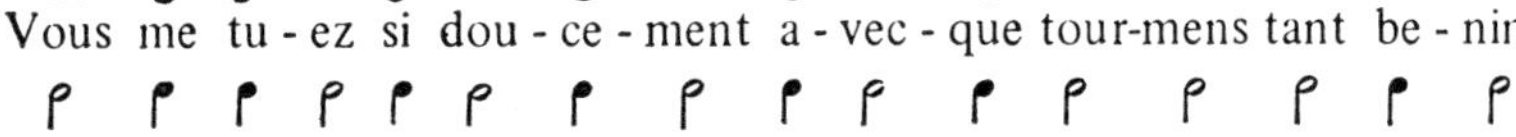

Long longer than short (F. Caietan)

— ◡ ◡ — ◡ — ◡ — ◡ — ◡ — — — ◡ —

Vous me tu - ez si dou - ce - ment, a - vec - que tour-mens tant be - nins

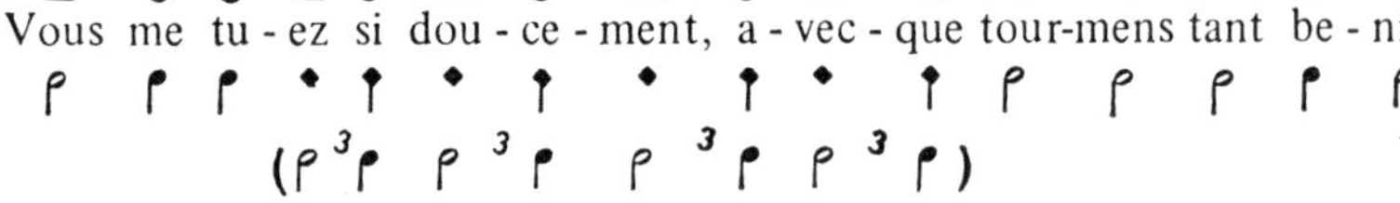

[21] See Masson, *op. cit.*, p. 1308.

[22] "The Aims of Baïf's Academy", *Musica Disciplina*, I (1946), p. 164.

[23] *Op. cit.*, p. 166.

[24] Based on Yates, *Academies...*, p. 54

Owing to the rigidity of the system, not very much music was written in the style of *vers mesurés à l'antique* and very little of it survives today.[25]

The choruses in the *Balet* are written in this "humanistic" style, in the more free manner, in which long notes are longer than short, but not always in an exact mathematical relation, using groups and occasional *hemiolia* to agree with the variations of French stress. If taken in this more flexible sense, the *vers mesurés* do correspond rather closely to the stress of French versa. However, this idea of long and short still presents all kinds of difficulties because in the pronunciation of French that differentiation is by no means clear or fixed, and this was true for the sixteenth century as well as for any other. The distinction between long and short as made by the sixteenth century french academician is often completely arbitrary. In the following example, from the Song of the Sirens, it can be readily seen that there is a little freedom in the matter of rhythm. In

— ∪ — — ∪ ∪ — — ∪ ∪ — ∪ — —
O - cé - an, pè - re che - nu, pè - re des Dieux re - con - nu, etc.

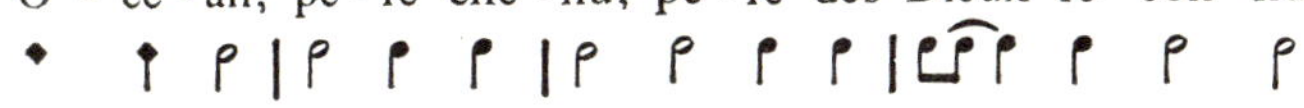

this notation the ♦♩ is equivalent to a triplet, ♩ ³ ♪, which equals the value of a long foot, or 𝅗𝅥, and fits the word "océan" admirably.[26]

It may be surprising that only the choral pieces are written in this new manner, the other items being in normal mensural music. This is due to the fact that all *musique mesurée* was written polyphonically, usually in 4 parts. It would have been expected that since the academicians were attempting to reproduce the music of the ancients their music would have been monodic. The explanation may be found in the preface to Claude Le Jeune's *Le Printemps*:

"... Since their [Orpheus' and Amphion's] time, Rhythm has been so neglected that she has been quite lost, whilst Harmony, for the last two hundred years has been so exactly sought out that she has been made

[25] The most important body of such works are the pieces in Claude Le Jeune's collection *Le Printemps*, 1603, pub. by H. Expert in *Maîtres musiciens de la Renaissance française*, parts 12-14, and the various songs by Jacques Mauduit, Thibaut de Courville, Eustache de Courroy, Guillaume Costeley and others in numerous anthologies of the early 17th century.

[26] "...the rhythm of the text [in the music of the *Balet comique*] is preserved to a remarkable degree, and there is good reason to suppose that the composers were consciously imitating *musique mesurée*." (Walker, "The Influence of musique mesurée à l'antique," *Musica Disciplina* II (1948) p. 144).

perfect, producing beautiful and grand effects but not such as those antiquity recounts. Which has caused astonishment to many, seeing that the ancients sang with one voice only, whereas we have the melody of several voices together . . . Claudin Le Jeune . . . was . . . bold enough to draw poor Rhythm out of the tomb where she had lain so long and to join her to Harmony... making [music] not only equal to that of the ancients, but much more excellent and more capable of beautiful effects, since it makes audible the body married to the soul, which till then had been separated..."[27]

One effect of this combination of words and music in which all parts pronounced the same syllable at the same time — in this respect different from ordinary polyphony of the period — was that it made the text completely audible. This was important in the view of the musical humanists, for they hoped that the union of the words, with their influence on the minds of men, and the music, with its influence on the souls of men, would produce effects similar to those attributed to ancient music.[28] It may be some such effect was indeed achieved, for D'Aubigné says that *vers mesurés*, when *sung*, has much grace, "as I have experienced in the great concerts given by the King's musicians".[29]

CAROL MACCLINTOCK

[27] Quoted from Walker, *Music Review* II (1940), p. 308.
[28] In this respect the *Balet* is closely related to other humanistically inspired theatrical works almost contemporary with it — the choruses written by A. Gabrieli for *Oedipus Rex*, performed at the Teatro Olimpico at Vicenza in 1585; the *intermedii* for *La Pellegrina*, of 1589; the two *Euridices*, Peri's and Caccini's, of 1600; and Cavalieri's *Rappresentazione di anima e di corpo* of the same year. The Florentine Camerata shared many of the humanistic ideas current in Baïf's Academy. Their requirements for treatment of the text were similar: intelligibility, declamation, relations between poetic meter and musical rhythm, *affetto della parola* which would influence the minds of the hearers. (See D. P. Walker, "La Musique des Intermèdes florentines de 1589", in *Les fêtes de la Renaissance*, C. N. R. S., 1965, p. 133 ff. Also Prunières, *op. cit.*, 106 et passim.)
[29] *Oeuvres*, *ed. cit.*, p. 273.

A word about the transcriptions:

In the transcriptions of the music here given, the normal stress of the French poetry has been the guide in barring the music, excepting, of course, the dances. This has led to rhythms which shift from 4/4 to 6/4 for the most part, but there are occasional 5/4 and 7/4 measures as well. In all of the music, again excluding the dances, the barring is not to be considered as indicating a heavy accent on the first beat; rather it should serve to guide the singers in proper stress groups. It is hoped that these renderings will have produced a musical transcription more faithful to the intent of the composers and avoid some of the impossible accents found in certain earlier transcriptions.

* * * * *

This translation was made from the facsimile edition published by the Bottega d'Erasmo, Turin, 1965:

> Balet comique de la Royne, faict aux nopces de Monsieur le Duc de Joyeuse & Madamoyselle de Vaudemont sa soeur. Par Baltasar de Beauioyeulx, valet de chambre du Roy, & de la Royne sa mere. A Paris, Par Adrian Le Roy, Robert Ballard, & Mamert Patisson, Imprimeurs du Roy. M.D.LXXXI.

We have translated the prose as faithfully as possible and have made no attempt to put into verse the translation of the poetic sections.

Grateful acknowledgement is due the University of Illinois Library for providing photographic copies of the Plates.

C. M. and L. M.

THE QUEEN'S COMEDY-BALLET

PRESENTED

on the occasion of the
marriage of her sister,

MADEMOISELLE DE VOUDEMONT

to the

DUC DE JOYEUSE

LE BALET COMIQUE DE LA ROYNE

by

BALTASAR DE BEAUJOYEULX,

Valet de Chambre to
THE KING, & THE QUEEN, HIS MOTHER

Paris,
Adrian le Roy, Robert Ballard, & Mamert
Patisson, Imprimeurs du Roy.
M. D. LXXXII.

TO THE KING OF FRANCE AND POLAND

SIRE, inasmuch as you, in handling the tiller of the French Empire, have achieved the two points of perfection of all human action — the practical and the pleasant — it seems more than just that your merits should be celebrated in both ways. For the practical, your conduct of armies, battles, engagements, sieges, taking of cities, trophies, journeys and sceptres, would be sufficient proof that Your Majesty has served the preservation, restoration, and grandeur of this crown. And in this regard, Sire, the history of France could provide you, not with equals, but with many seconds, kings, in truth, of great valor, honored by many fine conquests, and, after you, worthy of honor in all future centuries. But in the matter of pleasure — to have known how to temper this martial inclination with honest pleasures, delightful pastimes, recreation marvelous in variety, inimitable in beauty, incomparable in its delightful novelty — one will pardon me if I maintain that you have had no predecessor nor will ever have (as I believe) any successor.

Now as all these heroic facts may be devoured by inhuman Saturn with his teeth of oblivion, if they are not guaranteed by several defences and maintained by the protection of a noble account, likewise, all these delightful triumphs provided to give relaxation to your bellicose hand would return to their original obscurity and belittlement if they were not consigned to memory by discourse and pen. In dedicating this libretto to Your Majesty there is no more any need to state here, not the reasons but rather the necessities, than it would be to recount, in praise of the author of all things, these beautiful harmonies of the world that we see, these lovely variations the seasons produce, in short, all the happiness and contentment that we breathe in our low estate. Has Your Majesty wished to show how much sweetness, delectation and the good odor of peace you could shower on your people? Have you wished to refresh your nobility from so many military fatigues? Behold, a thousand pleasures and honest pastimes which appeared with dexterity, prompt to serve you, to make known to all neighboring kings, and to all more distant peoples, the loyalty and fertility and abundance of your kingdom, not only as to valiant men but also great and sensitive spirits. And after all your troubles you can amuse yourself among your subjects with more splendor and magnificence than other monarchs would have been able to do after a long peace and tranquillity. And as the excellent constitution and bearing of a person is seen, when, after some serious illness there still remains in him a disposition that the strongest and hardest would try in vain to imitate, so, after many disorders that you have experienced, to see so great an affluence of good humor, so *gaillard* a disposition of good will and such kind understanding to bring about that which you desired — this will serve as a true and infallible sign of the good and solid establishment of your kingdom.

Also, I do not wish here to withold honor from those who have treated and watched the malady, particularly in this palace the Queen, your Mother, who has kept vigil so many nights, kept busy so many days, given so many wise counsels, and applied so many salutary remedies, that at last the healing has followed and fresh color has returned to your France, the good appetite to serve you faithfully, arms and legs robust to sustain you, heart and mind healthy to cause peace to revive and to blossom.

The telling of all this, Sire, is here, vividly and agreeably represented in the narration of the sorceress Circe, whom you have won by your virtue with greater praise than Ulysses, of whom the great Alexander was envious for having been so worthily celebrated by Homer. In sum, this will be your poetic, or, if you like better, your comic [theatrical] history, which will bring your renown to all manner of men, even those who would not seek out serious matters. You will be found with Jove, along with most of the gods and goddesses, I mean divine help, exterminating the enchantment of vice. So your name, Sire, will live forever, perfumed by the grateful odor not only of virtuous reputation but also of pleasant delectation.

Begging Your Majesty most humbly, that since you found the execution of my little design — among so many other fine, superb representations — agreeable, that the memory which I hope to perpetuate and communicate, by means of this little volume, to those who have not seen it, you may find it worthy of recommendation. And, like the delightful viands that one season denies to another, or of which one country has the advantage over its neighbors, by means of canning are preserved and transported and bring admiration and benediction to the lands where they are grown, so this confection of spirit that you have found pleasant, and which will not grow again except in the country obedient to you, preserved in the sugar of your good graces, seasoned by your contentment, and sealed in the container of this little monument, may give a taste to all nations of the nectar and ambrosia for which you are reputed, and also whet the appetites of your people; without, however, the true taste ever coming to others than to those who have considered, through the splendor of Your Majesty, presiding in the midst of so many rarities and sumptuousities, and without anyone being able to imagine the beautiful order of so great a number of diversities, so many different, nonetheless excellent and living beauties, and so many admirable voices, both for reciting and singing. This, which in truth, Sire, belongs only to your grandeur, will never weary you, nor can anyone, however great he may be, expect to be able to equal it. The preeminence in this dwells in Your Majesty, as the precedence of your dignity surpasses all the other Christian kings. Invoking, therefore, the universal Father, so kind and indulgent, that it may please Him to continue His grace and these contentments to you, until such an age when one can say of Your Majesty:

And you will see of your race
Double posterity;
And on the French, grace,
Peace, and felicity.

Your most humble and obedient servant
and subject
De Beaujoyeulx

HENRICO III. REGI FRAN-
corum et Polonorum
Christianissimo

QUI ficto falso labentes aethere spectant,
Rex *Henrice*, deos, tanti mirantur amántque
Artificis, bellè qui fingit ludicra, mirum
Ingenium: Tua te sed quàm miratur amátque
Gallia tota magis? Nec enim conficta, sed ipsa
Vera Astraea suis ad te descendit ab astris:
Et tua ne victos se transfuga vertat ad hostes,
En tibi praecisas Victoria consecrat alas.
Haec spectacula te ducunt, haec seria curas,
Seria, quae seri poterunt meminisse nepotes.
Allicis è caelo non tu simulachra deorum,
Quae deducta manu tibi BELLOIOIUS offert:
At, quibus es charus, miris virtutibus ipsos
Praesentes, verósque deos (Rex optime) vero
In tam foelices dimettis ab aethere terras.

Eliciúmne Iovem summa deduxit ab arce
Sic Numa Rex, licet hunc Faunus, Picúsque iuvarent?
Qua fulmen tandem posset ratione piari
Hic pius & supplex tremula tum voce rogabat.
Iuppiter ocyus, ut caecis oracula verbis
Involuit, refugit celeres iratus in auras.
Sed tibi (Rex *Henrice*) volens delapsus ab alto
Iuppiter est caelo: docuit quibus artibus illa,
Quorum iamdudum miserè tua Gallia flagrans
Ardebat flammis, extinguere fulmina posses.
His abeat numquam tam magnus sedibus hospes
Iuppiter optamus. Nam si discedit, in altum
Te metuo pariter secum ne tollat olympum.

A. Pogoesaeus

TO THE SIEUR DE BEAUJOYEUX UPON THE QUEEN'S COMEDY-BALLET

Beaujoyeux, you who first bring back from the ashes of Greece the plan and accomplishments of the ballet, who ever outdo yourself in divine spirit; mathematician, inventive, alone in your knowledge, if ever honor is deserved, yours is assured.

What an honor to be the only one who makes us worthy, by so many inventions, so many remarkable stories, who brought to fruition in a single day the plans of a great king; an equal of Archimedes in joining the practical to the theoretical, he during a storm, you during better times, free from war and fear!

Minerva, whom you portray as triumphing, as an enemy of Circe, who pours into our minds the potion of vice and its deceptive appearance, Minerva seems to me to be none other than this great Princess, wife of a great King, the very essence of wisdom, who destroys vice with the scythe of her greatness.

As she shines, divine, in her royal soul, as she has triumphed over wicked Circe, so may she soon be mother of a fine Dauphin. Only this is lacking for her to be completely happy, that alone promises good fortune for her and for her beauties, companions of Destiny!

Billard

* * * *

My mind, (Beaujoyeux) is lost completely in your lofty learned plans, snatched from the ancient monuments of Greece to entertain our Kings with so rare a spectacle. The Scythians, who have hearts of stone, would stare at such a sweet miracle, and their captured hearts would no longer be stained with the bitter humor of barbarian pride. Your Circe, Beaujoyeux, does not charm me as much as the subtle figures of your ballet, the more so as the magic of your Circe yields to the heavenly Moly.[1] But I feel my soul enchanted by such sweet pleasures, and all my senses so ravished, that even Mercury could scarcely find the remedy.

Auguste Costé, Dunoisien

Beneath the vault, shining with azure and flame enamel, how many beautiful spirits I perceive whom a holy Daemon leads and conducts! There is nothing so difficult but that their work will do honor to our world, combining both the pleasurable and the useful.

Your mind, my dear Beaujoyeux, as gay as it is beautiful, by a new invention gives pleasure to earth and heaven. You set yourself gently apart from the crude and vulgar crowd by your good, sane judgment. Not everyone can do this.

Time, which spoils and breaks everything, can never destroy so learned and rich a work, and will never see the end of it. (How powerful is excellence!) Time will see himself forced to maintain so fine a work for our children yet to be born.

So many spirits one sees scattered about, who think they are happy in this world, having neither knowledge nor skill from fertile nature, are blind to the light, are beggars with possessions. He who has knowledge is like a King who has never known poverty.

For a lofty plan one must have lofty things. But if one makes a few mistakes all are disappointed. What could one imagine greater, more lofty, newer, than the plan which your beautiful conception has made you undertake?

No envious person could belittle your perfect and great work. You have given no cause for derision either to the learned or the ignorant. But by means of painting joined to nature, your work showed itself such that art has surpassed nature.

1 Moly - a fabulous herb, according to Homer, with black root and white blossom, used by Mercury to counteract Circe's spell upon Ulysses.

To the eyes of my Prince, Henry, who will undo his enemies from Pole to Pole, since he is favored by high Heaven, you have been able to show virtue in the very person of Virtue, played by the lady who wears a diadem on her head.

You have been able to show cleverly that beneath its attractive covering vice no longer has power when virtue has been encountered. By your admirable wit you made night into day, and of the Winter a continuing Springtime.

You show us without danger the prized wealth of the Indies; and the highly esteemed manner of our ancient poets, verses with music, the complicated ballet brought into order, showing by a mystical effect the unity of the blue heavens.

Because you tried great and diverse things, you, as did the Persians, have invented this new ballet. One constructs what is great from a prudent and perfect mind. Such fruits are rarely sold; he who buys them is lucky.

The prize one gives a virtuous man, for such a worthy exchange, is the gold of lofty praise, which you deserve, Beaujoyeux. A noble soul always prefers honor to profit or gain. May you have as your reward this treasure which is more divine than human.

Alla gran virtù non si può dare altro
premio che la gloria e la laude.

Volusian

TO THE READER

Although, friend Reader, the title and inscription of this book is unusual, and although one has never before seen a Ballet printed, nor the word "comic" adapted to it, I beg you to regard neither the one nor the other as strange. For, as to the Ballet, even though it may be a modern invention, or at least repeated so far distant from antiquity that it can be so called, being, in truth, only some geometric mixtures of several persons dancing together to a diverse harmony of several instruments, I confess to you that simply represented by [means of visual] impression it would have had much novelty, and little beauty, the recitation of a simple comedy. Also it would have been neither very excellent nor worthy of such a great queen, who wished to do something truly magnificent and triumphant. Because of this I decided it would not be a bad idea to mix one and the other together and to diversify the music with poetry and weave music into the poetry, and most often to merge the two together; for in antiquity they never recited poetry without music, and Orpheus never played without words. I have, however, given first place and honor to the dance, and second place to the substance, which I have called "comic" more for the beautiful, tranquil and happy conclusion than for the quality of the personages, who are almost all gods and goddesses, or other heroic persons. Thus I have animated and made the Ballet speak, and Comedy sing and resound, and have added many rare and rich scenes and ornaments. I may say that within a single well-proportioned body I have pleased eye, ear, and mind. I beg you, from the novelty of it or from the title, not to judge it badly; for the invention being composed principally of these two parts, I could not attribute all to the Ballet without wronging the Comedy, distinctly represented by its scenes and acts, nor to the Comedy without prejudice to the Ballet, which honors, enlivens and fills out the sense of the Comedy with harmonious recitation. So that, having been well-advised to inform you abundantly of my intentions, I beg you also not to take fright at the name, and take it all in good part, since I have desired, for my part, to satisfy you.

* * *

BALET COMIQUE DE LA ROYNE

The King, having concluded and fixed the marriage between Monsieur the Duke de Joyeuse, peer of France, and Mademoiselle de Vaudemont, sister of the Queen, decided to solemnize the wedding by all kinds of triumphs and magnificences to honor such a fine couple, in keeping with their valor and merit. To effect this, in addition to the rich costumes and apparatus, delightful entertainments and sumptuous mascarades, his Majesty ordered also different kinds of races, and superb combats of arms, at the Barrier as well as in the Lists, on foot and on horseback, conducted in the manner of the ancient Greeks and of some nations who today are the most distant from us. All of this was accompanied by musical concerts, excellent and never before heard, his Majesty wishing to omit nothing that might entertain with the most delightful variety the illustrious company invited to these ceremonies.

All of these plans were carried out to the great admiration and astonishment of those present, who began then to believe that the magnificences and triumphs which took place on similar occasions in the courts of the greatest kings and emperors, recounted by the ancient Romans, were much less, on the whole, than those which they had enjoyed. But in all these public acts, and chiefly in the military exercises, this great King, according to the common opinion of the Ambassadors, won so much esteem and victory over the princes and lords of his realm that he seemed to be born of himself with even more glory and grandeur, making thus a declaration that he was truly worthy of the name of King, which Cyrus said belonged only to those who in all virtuous and praiseworthy things excelled those they were able to command. On this point, however, the spectators remained in perplexity as to how to judge truly whether the plans of his Majesty to honor the solemnity of the wedding or the willingness of the princes and lords to execute them was the greater. For while it is the custom of his Majesty to conceive great things, it appears nevertheless that the result of these high conceptions cannot redound so greatly to his reputation as the great expense which the Nobility went to voluntarily (to obey and please him) merits praise, having shown by their deportment how much they could be prodigal of their goods and their very lives when it was a question of preservation of the crown and the state.

The Queen, seeing so many preparations being made to honor her sister's marriage, and that all vied with one another to give pleasure and to content the King, the Queen-Mother and herself, she resolved herself to do something worthy of his Majesty.

Since she does me the honor of finding not disagreeable the inventions which I sometimes propose to her in affairs like these, she sent for me at my home. I set off immediately to cast myself at her feet and pay her my very humble respects. As soon as I arrived at court her Majesty took the trouble to inform me of a good part of the arrangements which had already been decided on, and commanded me to draw up a plan for her which would yield in no way to the other preparations either in beauty of subject or in the arrangement and carrying out of the work. She said she wanted to assist in it and even take part, so that by decorating and honoring the festival in this manner she would let the whole world know that she yielded to no one in affection and good will for those for whom these preparations were being made.

After having received this definite command, I immediately went into retirement so that, far from the noisy court, I would be able with more peace and freedom of mind, to satisfy the wish and intention of her Majesty. After having applied all my strength for several days, I finally decided on the plan which has since been carried out. When I had written it out I immediately went back to the court to present it to the Queen and to learn from her Majesty if my work and industry had fulfilled her wish and satisfied her. Her Majesty, after having me read the discourse in the presence of several princesses and ladies who were with her — when my work had been examined, commanded me to carry out my plan forthwith.

Whereupon I remonstrated that my plan was composed of three parts, that is, verse which must be recited, different musical compositions which must be sung, and a variety of things which must be presented in painting. As for the poetry, I said, I was well aware of my small competence, and that, to tell the truth, I had inserted some verses in my discourse not to be recited but only to serve as a suggestion for some learned and excellent poet to write others worthy to be uttered in so grand a company as was to be honored by such great majesty, and by the greatest and rarest minds of the century. Then, too, as for the music, diversity was so necessary, that it would be impossible to be satisfactory in the little time remaining; still less to represent the necessary things in painting.

Not being able to supply all these three things at once, I humbly asked her Majesty to give the charge for poetry, music, and painting to persons who could acquit themselves worthily. Then her Majesty, having considered what I proposed so that she might be better served and better contented by the carrying out of the work, commanded Lord La Chesnaye, the King's Almoner, to compose the poems upon subjects which I would give to him. Also she commanded Lord de Beaulieu (who is her servant) to set up in his apartment everything which might be termed perfect in music upon the ideas which I would communicate to him, connected with the subject matter of the plot. He bore himself so well in this matter that he (who, the best musicians say, excells in the art) really surpassed himself. He was helped at all times by the musicians of the King's Chamber and especially by Maître Salmon, whom de Beaulieu and other knowledgeable persons rightly esteem highly in this art.

As for the paintings, I employed at the Queen's command Jacques Patin, the King's painter, who has acquitted himself of the task as well as any painter in the kingdom could, by finishing the work, difficult as it was, in the few days to which necessity forced us. The works and accomplishments of the people I have mentioned, brought much praise from understanding persons, without their needing praise from such a sterile pen as I wield. Nevertheless, I could not and ought not to suppress what is due them. Also, because what is praiseworthy should always be exalted and prized, I feared that by keeping silent about the merits of those men I had to use, they might accuse me of trying to use other people's pens to their detriment, since everyone is anxious to keep the fruits from his own garden.

I, myself, who am ignorant of the law, could perfectly well find those that have been passed against plagiarism, if someone tried to steal my own creations, which I think always do me honor, since they have pleased the greatest queen in the world. Besides, I can somewhat participate in the honor they are given because I am aware of their capabilities[2] which they have employed in the service of the Queen, using my subjects and my inventions. These can have more appreciation and can be more readily imagined if, first of all, by pictures and by descriptions I depict the preparations and the machinery that I had constructed in the Great Salle Bourbon [of the Louvre], the place where my inventions were staged and carried out.

* * *

First of all, you must imagine that around the hall there are two galleries, one above the other, with gilded armrests and balustrades and at the eastern end you can see a semicircle. There I had a dais constructed near the floor, with three degrees of height, the whole width of the room. This was to be used only for the seats of the King, the Queen Mother, princes and princesses. In front of this dais on either side there were two seats intended for the Ambassadors; and behind, forty wooden steps the whole width of the room, rising as far as the first of the galleries. These seats were used by the ladies and the damsels of the court. All around the lower part of the hall there were steps rising as far as the upper gallery. (Plate I).

On the right side, the side where his King's Majesty was, and in the middle of the hall, there was set up a small grove of trees, eighteen feet long and twelve feet wide. It was sacred to Pan, the god of shepherds, and was a woodland raised a foot and a half from the floor, in perspective, higher in the back than the front. All around it were fine oak trees two feet apart, whose trunks, leaves, and acorns were gilded and made with great skill. At regular intervals in these trees there was a small niche, to seat the Dryads when they should appear. Behind the grove, against the wall, I had a cave built as dark as the hollow in some real rock. It shone and reflected out-

[2] *I. e.* Salmon, Beaulieu, and Patin.

side as if a vast number of diamonds had been inserted in it. It was in addition decorated and embellished with trees, and covered with flowers, amid which you could see leopards and other animals so cleverly imitated that one would have said they were alive and natural. The ground of the wood was also carpeted with grass and flowers and with a multitude of rabbits running ceaselessly from one end to the other. In the middle, before the cave, was a mound of earth rising directly in front of the grotto. Here was seated the god Pan, dressed as a satyr, enveloped in a mantle of cloth of gold, with a golden crown on his head, holding in his left hand a knobby and spiny club, and in his right hand his gilded Pan-pipes, upon which he played at the right moment. Inside the cave, behind thc door, was set up the regal organ, to be played at the right time and place. Also all of the trees were laden with oil lamps, made like little boats, gilded with pure gold, whose wicks shed light upon all sides, for the wood was veiled by a curtain made so cleverly that instead of adding to the obscurity it served, on the contrary, as a light, to show more naturally all that the woodland contained.

Across from the grove, on the King's left, was constructed a wooden vault, eighteen feet long and nine wide, with an opening in its front only three feet long. Outside it was covered all over with fat clouds, and inside covered with gold which shone and glittered because of the numerous lights hidden in it; they made the gold shine so that the place seemed to be a part of the blue sky. Inside the vault there were ten concerts of music, all different. And this vault was called "golden" both because of its splendor and on account of the music which was performed in it. This music, because of the repercussive voices, was thought by some of those present to be the same voice converted into repercussive air, once called Echo. Others more learned in Platonic philosophy thought it was the true harmony of heaven, by which all living things are conserved and maintained.

Between the woodland and the vault, overhead was a fat cloud full of stars whose light pierced the cloud. Through this Mercury and Jupiter were to descend to Earth.

At the other end of the room, opposite the King, an artificial garden was constructed, located in the middle of the hall, extending in front to a width of three fathoms, in the rear twelve feet, raised a foot from the ground in front and three feet in the rear. This garden was enclosed in a balustrade covered with fine gold and burnished silver, and was divided in four parts by two green *allées*. Each quarter had a border; one of lavender, another of aspic, a third of rosemary, and a fourth of sage. The ground of these divisions was embellished with all diverse sorts of flowers, and also strawberries, cucumbers, melons, and all sorts of those little fruits that grow close to the soil. And at the two sides of the garden one perceived rare and exquisite fruit trees, like oranges, grenadines, lemons, and apples. Every tree was loaded with fruit, with the same grace and pleasure that Nature gives to everything she produces, all being imitated in gold, silver, silk and feathers of the necessary colors. The garden was made even more beautiful by a vaulted trellis, from which one could see hanging fine large grapes, so cleverly made that one might take them for real, and Nature herself seemed astonished at the handiwork.

At the top of this trellis before the garden was to be seen a great sun of polished gold, with golden rays, which one would have said was the real cause of the growth of the fruits and the other things reproduced so naturally. At the rear of the garden there were two sturdy towers at the two sides, whose stones were cut in diamond shape, crenelated all around, and from their tops streamed fine and rich streamers. Between the towers was the wall of the castle, armed with its crenelations and defenses. At the bottom, and at the middle of the gate of the castle, which projected a foot and a half, there was a vault, made in imitation of a conch shell or sea-needle. The most beautiful part of this vault was that it was pierced with round holes set with glass of all kinds of colors. Behind these glass panes shone the same number of oil lamps, which cast a hundred thousand colors upon the garden through the transparent glass.

The door was also covered with gold and vari-colored paintings so rich that they dazzled viewers, who could not find the source of light and, still less, of the variety of the colors. Behind the wall one could perceive the perspective of a city with towers in the middle. The whole affair was arranged so cleverly that one could imagine streets and fields in the distance.

Outside the garden on either side were two vaulted trellises fifteen feet long and twenty-four high, with leaves and fine grapes which appeared natural. This place was the more remarkable because through it must pass the musicians for the intermedi and the vehicles which were to appear before the King.

Now this garden was the place where Circe, the enchantress, had her abode. She was seated in the gate of the castle, clad in a golden robe of two colors, decorated all over with small tufts of gold and silk, and she wore a veil of silver and silk crêpe; the adornments of her head, neck and arms being marvellously enriched with precious stones and pearls of inestimable worth. In her hand she bore a golden wand five feet long, one just like the one the ancient Circe used to bear, when, by a touch of this wand, she used to convert men into beasts and into inanimate objects. This Circe, so celebrated by the poets, was played by Mademoiselle de Sainte Mesme. She lived (as we have said) in this garden where there were a hundred wax candles, emitting such light, shining so upon the fairy and the garden, that the eyes of the spectators were dazzled. In addition, the infinity of tapers which were at the top and all around the room gave forth such brilliant light as to put to shame the finest and calmest day of the year.

The fifteenth of October, a Sunday, was the day appointed to act out, after the preparation described above, the plot which follows. Since everybody wanted to feast his eyes upon the things which rumor had already described as very great, if not as magnificent, superb and admirable as they have been esteemed after the performance, and every curious person was desirous of seeing the use of such great and magnificent machines — as early as daybreak one saw all sorts of people crowding around the doors of the hall. Though the doors were strictly guarded by the archers of the King's guard, by lieutenants and bailiffs who let in only well-known persons of rank, nonetheless when the King, in the Company of the Queen Mother, princes and princesses, lords and ladies of the court, entered the hall one could easily count nine or ten thousand spectators there.

* * *

When their Majesties, princes, princesses, lords and ladies, kings, ambassadors and foreign princes had been seated in the chairs and places prepared for each, according to his rank as described above, about ten o'clock in the evening, when silence had been imposed, one heard from behind the castle the sound of oboes, trumpets, sackbuts, and other sweet musical instruments. When their harmony had ceased, Lord de la Roche (a gentleman serving the Queen Mother, clad in silver cloth, his garment covered with precious stones and pearls) — Lord de la Roche, coming from Circe's garden, ran into the middle of the room. Stopping there, he turned his frightened face toward Circe's garden to see if the enchantress were following. When he saw that no one was pursuing him, he drew from his pocket a kerchief embroidered with gold, with which he wiped his face as though he were perspiring with fatigue and fright. Then, somewhat reassured, he walked slowly toward the King and, having made a deep bow to his Majesty, began, with assured demeanor and in language full of sage eloquence, to speak as follows.

SPEECH OF THE FUGITIVE GENTLEMAN TO THE KING

Some catastrophe always opposes that which favorable Heaven proposes to send to mortals, and the man who has too great a desire to do good is deceived by hope. I wanted to be the first to announce the news that the inhuman and cruel Age of Iron was changing to a better age and that the gods, who with Saturn remained on earth, were coming to France to dwell with mortals, to ornament the country forever with peace and abundance. But whom (oh Gods!) did I encounter when I drew near? Oh Gods! Deflect the evil onto her wicked head!

It was a woman; no breathing being has so much beauty and so much evil! In her wild eyes the sun shone — eyes where hidden Cupid sharpened his golden darts. Her complexion was lily-white and rose-red. But beneath such beauty poison was hidden, which flowed from her mouth in honeyed words to trap the hearts of those she desired. As soon as I saw her, I saw my liberty and almost my life taken from me. Careful of her pleasures, as she came toward me, she spoke thus:

Stop, oh Knight! Be not afraid and come near; and if your heart is not made of wood or stone, obey without resisting the laws of that Archer-god who rules everywhere; and whom (perhaps) you would resist in vain, for he dominates the very gods, who, subject to his power, just as I am now, feel his sharp arrows. Overcome by your eyes, I surrender to you alone. I know that I am not unworthy to be loved, I, Circe, famous everywhere for my art, who can subject the sceptres of kings, who can deprive men of their will, who, with their bodies changed into monstrous forms, endure at my pleasure my harsh prison. And in my palace of white marble, studded with diamonds, with gilded floor, full of lovely furnishings for my daily use, I use only nymphs to do the labor. They are wood nymphs, and nymphs of the small streams, of the great rivers which deliver their waters to the depths of the seas and wake with their waves their sister Nereids sleeping in Tethys' dwelling. I do not wish to change you into a monster with my wand. You have some destiny which forces me to love you. Come share my possessions, employ my wealth, and make use of these goddesses just as I do.

I followed her! — for there is no stronger attraction than the anticipation of pleasure and well-being. There I dwelt happily (if he who allows himself to be ruled by pleasure can be called happy), until an evil Fate full of harshness and hate and suspicion poisoned Circe's heart against me. In a trice she turned against me and, smiting my breast with her golden wand, transformed all my members into the body of a lion, and locked me up with her flock in a pen. But for some reason the witch softened and returned me to my original form. Now, so as not to fall again under her cruel rule (who dares subject himself to her charms more than once?) I tried to escape while she had mounted to the top of a tower in a state of agitation which had made her distrust her own power. She had gone to spy upon the nymphs from afar so as to prevent them by a magic spell from seeing that King who is summoning them to a temple in France, together with other gods who are bringing the Golden Age down from heaven.

Crueler than a serpent whose back the fleeing peasant breaks with a stick, her eye is fiery, and fear, struggling with her suspicious hope, fills her breast. I have come to that King who has assumed the defense of the gods — I have come swiftly to denounce the plot and ask his help against Circe.

Oh great King, are you not willing to aid so many gods? You will do it, Henry, braver than Alcide, or the hero who slew the deadly Chimera, and because of the many mortals and gods whom you will deliver from the fairy's bonds, you will make yourself immortal, and posterity, which will erect temples to you, will crown your brow with the verdant laurel.

When his speech had ended, he knelt before the King, as though putting himself under his protection. Now, behold Circe issuing from her garden with her wand raised in her hand! She came quickly to the middle of the room, looking in every direction for the fugitive gentleman who had escaped from her prison. Raising her eyes toward the hanging cloud, with a sad voice and a grace which few damsels could rival and none could surpass, she began to lament, as follows.

LAMENT OF CIRCE FOR HAVING LOST A GENTLEMAN

In vain I pursue him! He has escaped and I have no hope of ever renewing my power over him. Alas! Circe, what have you done? You should never remake into a man a person you have deprived of his reason. Circe, you are not very smart or clever. Be warned by this mistake of yours. This fugitive, free, will depart fearless, and will everywhere spread abroad your shame. In vain do you use your spells on your captives. In vain do you change them by magical words, since you are changeable and since pity and ruthlessness each possess a half of you.

Silly, three times silly Circe, silly and frivolous. You think that a man who has returned to his original state will consent to love you afterward, and will allow himself to be deluded by pleasure, when he can use his reason?

Root out the pity which makes you changeable. Good becomes harmful when it does damage. Follow your own nature alone! Wrath and cruelty are your traits, kindness is right for others.

Circe! divest yourself of this cowardice. Arm your heart with serpents and rage. Let no one whom you have smitten with your wand ever boast that he escaped from your yoke.

As soon as she had poured out her wrath in this lament, she returned to her garden, looking like a very angry woman. When she had left the room, those present were astounded at the two acts they had seen — the fugitive gentleman and the irate Circe.

When silence had been restored, lo, one of the floats entered, three Sirens and a Triton; draped over their arms were their tails covered with scales of gold and polished silver, the tails, fins, and hanging flippers of burnished gold; their body-covering and hair, which hung down to their waists, were laced with gold thread, and each carried a golden mirror. In this equipage they entered the hall singing the following song: at each verse one of the groups of musicians in the golden vault answered singing. (Plate II).

Song of the Sirens Music p. 45)

Bearded father Ocean, recognized father of Gods,
already Triton is hitching his ceaselessly-moving chariot;
shall we issue forth from our waters where this Triton
calls us?
 — Go, daughters of Achelaus, follow the Triton who calls you.
  Tune your voices to his horn and sing the immortal
   praise of a great King.

One sees the chorus of the sister Nereids issue forth from
the waves and depart with Tethys; Doris carefully combing
the wet hair of silver-footed Tethys.
 — Go, daughters...

Jupiter is not alone in the sky, the sea contains a thousand
gods; one king alone dwells in France, Henry, great King of
the French. He yields to no god as to people, justice, or laws.
 — Go, daughters...

The lily when it blooms white is the honor of a fine garden;
the pine tree is king of the woods; this great King appears
thus among the other kings in good fortune and in courage.
 — Go, daughters...

Jupiter has divided the heavens where he dwells and also the
earth into equal parts. Jupiter will possess the heavens and
this great King will enjoy faithful Gaul in peace.
 — Go, daughters...

Tethys stops at the sound of Glaucus, who is touching the
strings of his lyre with his fingers; let us listen to his
song — he seems to be lamenting and his dolphin is sighing.
 — Go, daughters...

LE CHANT DES SEREINES

RÉPONSE DE LA VOUTE DORÉE

The marine monsters made the whole circuit of the hall, then retired near the trellis, where they encountered a beautiful fountain which one can truthfully call the most beautiful as to construction and art, magnificence of enrichment, that has ever been seen. A description of it will make every person of judgment share this opinion. So I wish particularly to insert at this point its description and its picture. (See Plate III).

Its first basin was twelve feet in diameter and seven feet high, made with twelve panels, on each of which there were two Tritons and Nereids with their long tails. They bore in their hands musical instruments and were swimming in the sea. Above their heads and the panels there were children, who by a clever artifice had their cheeks puffed out, ready to squirt out the water from the basin. All of this was carved in relief, made of burnished gold, the water of burnished silver, imitating this element so closely that it seemed to be the waters of a placid river.

Above this basin was an edging, projecting one foot, and another small basin was formed by this projection, large enough, however, to receive the whole decoration of the fountain. Around and above this basin there were twelve seats, whose balustrades were formed of dolphins' tails made of burnished gold, and in the middle of the basin were to be seen three large dolphins in a trough, their muzzles downwards in the basin, their tails upwards. With their tails they supported another basin, eight feet in diameter, with sirens, tritons, and faces of children in relief, all covered with gold. In the middle of this basin were three additional dolphins who bore on their tails another smaller basin, four feet in diameter, carved in relief like the first one, and in it could be seen three other dolphins together, with tails twisted in the form of a pyramid. At the apex of this pyramidal union of tails there was a large ball five feet in diameter and around it six faces of six babies equally spaced. The ball, the faces, and the dolphins were of burnished gold and silver, and the ball was full of perfumed water, expelled through the children's mouths, and falling from the first basin to the second, to the larger third. There all this water fell upon the feet of the twelve

Naiads, who were sitting in the gold chairs we have described, with their feet in the water.

Foremost among them was the Queen, who because of her bearing, mien, gravity and royal majesty, seemed to be rather something divine and immortal than something human and mortal. After her there were Miladies the Princess of Lorraine, the Duchesses of Mercueil, Guyenne, Nevers, Aumalle, and Joyeuse; the Maréchales of Raiz and of l'Archant; also Miladies de Pons, de Bourdeille and de Cypierre. They were all seated in the golden seats, representing those water-nymphs called Naiads by the ancient poets. They were dressed in cloth of silver, enriched by veils of silver and red, which billowed around their sides and around their bodies, and at all the ends [of the veils] small tufts of gold and scarlet silk added grace to their apparel. Their heads were decorated with little triangles set with diamonds, rubies, pearls, and other exquisite precious stones; also their necks and arms were garnished with collars, chokers, and bracelets, and their clothes were covered with jewels, which shone and sparkled as do the stars at night in the azure mantle of the firmament. On the arms of the Queen's seat were two dolphins, sustaining by their tails a great golden crown, suspended above the head of her Majesty. Under the large basin, in front were figured three sea horses, or hippopotamus, pulling the fountain, swimming in water. They were six feet long, of burnished gold, and the water was burnished silver. On either side of their tails were two other seats, in one of which sat the Sieur de Beaulieu, representing Glaucus, called by poets the Sea God; in the other sat Mme. de Beaulieu, his wife, holding a lute in her hand, and representing Tethys, Goddess of the Sea. Both were dressed magnificently in robes of white satin, embroidered with foil, and their head-dresses were those with which gods and goddesses are depicted.

On either side of these two, eight Tritons with long tails were marching. Their bodies and tails were covered with scales of gold and polished silver, and their beards and wigs laced with gold thread. The Tritons were acted by the King's chamber singers, playing on lutes, harps, flutes and other instruments, and singing also. (Pl. IV). On both sides of the large basin marched twelve pages dressed in white satin enriched with gold foil, each of whom carried in his hands two large tapers of white wax. In addition to these lights, around the edge of the basin, the seats, and the dolphins of the fountain, there were a hundred tapers of white wax, each two feet long. All this splendor converted the darkness of the night into a great joyous light and made the water of the fountain, represented by gold and silver, dazzle the eyes of the spectators by its brilliance.

As soon as the Sirens saw this troupe of Sea Gods, they joined the group, and entering the hall, the fountain began to move toward the king's throne, to the sound of music from instruments and voices. These were the words —

Song of the Tritons (Music, p. 50.)

Come, faithful companions, let each of us weave a crown
with fresh leaves and white flowers for her perfumed head.
Here comes Tethys on a sea-shell in place of her silver
chariot. She has brought a crown to present to Louise,
her chariot and her trident. Our troupe is faithful to
immortal Tethys, and to Louise, who unites in her person
all the virtues, and who should reign here.

As soon as this fine company had appeared before their Majesties this music ceased and then Glaucus and Tethys began to sing the following dialogue. At the end of each couplet the whole band of Tritons answered, repeating the last line, as follows:

Gl. What good, Tethys, is this new shell, now that I have
been changed from a fisherman into a sea-god? I would
like not to be a god, but to be loved by Scylla, so as
not to be consumed by a cruel fire.

Te. Cupid's bow is all-conquering over gods and men, and the
wounds of his darts bring the same suffering to all who are smitten.
— Chorus: And the wounds of his darts... etc.

Gl. I became immortal because I ate an herb. I felt the
strength and power of the herb. Hoping to receive some
aid against Love I went to envious and proud Circe.

Te. The enflamed heart is never so much irritated as when it
has offered itself vainly and has suffered a shameful rejection.
— Cho. As when...

LA MUSIQUE DES TRITONS

Read: al-lé-gres-se for al-le-gres-se

GLAUCUS — THETUS

(All the stanzas are to be sung to this melody,
except the last, which is interlocutory.)

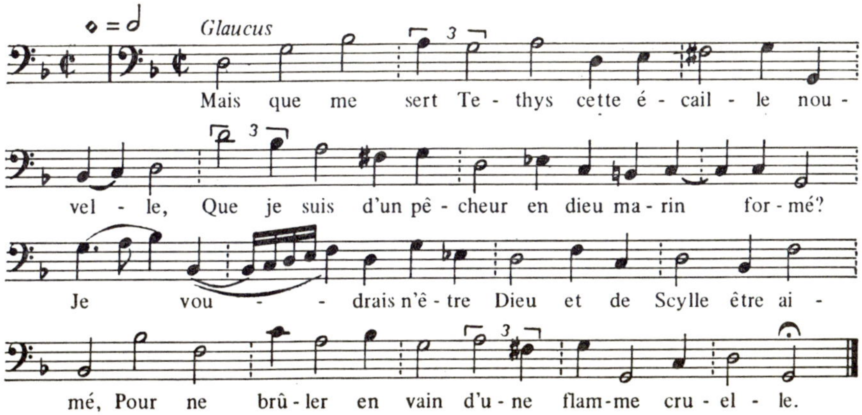

Et de ses traits la bles - sure à cha - cun Qui
Et de ses traits la bles - sure à cha - cun Qui
Contra
Et de ses traits la bles - sure à cha - cun Qui
Tenor
Et de ses traits la bles - sure à cha - cun Qui
Bassus
Et de ses traits la bles - sure à cha - cun Qui
la re - çoit ap - porte un mal com - mun
la re - çoit ap - porte un mal com - mun.
la re - çoit ap - porte un mal com mun.
la re - çoit ap - porte un mal com - mun.
la re - çoit ap - porte un mal com - mun

Glaucus
Et qui
est cet - te nym - phe? Est - ceu - ne ne -
Tethys
re - i - de? Non, car la mer n'a
point tel - le nym - phe con - çeu.
Gl.
Je sais bien c'est Ve - - nus.
Te.
Tu es en - cor dé - çue, El - le a chas - sé Ve - nus
Gl.
dans les jar - dins de Gni - de. C'est donc Ju - non.
Te.
Gl.
Tu te dé - çois. Est - ce la Ju - non des Fran-çais?
Te.
Ce n'est Ju - non; c'est Lou - i - se, et son nom pas -
se en pou-voir tous les noms
de Ju - non.

Gl. The forests will cover the whole sea with shade, sooner than Scylla shall be torn from my heart. Come, Dolphin, I wish to search for Scylla. Compassionate Dolphin, cleave the waves and swim.

Te. Circe has by her venom changed your Scylla into a rock as far as her waist, and her feet buried in the water have been transformed into dogs.
— Cho. And her feet...

Gl. Circe, jealous Circe, unworthy to be daughter of the god who controls the great flame in the sky, do you dare to enchant gods, you who were accustomed to enchant only men?

Te. Animate bodies are transformed by Circe into monsters when they have tasted her poison while deprived of their reason.
— Cho. When they have tasted...

Gl. The gods have the prayers of humans, who pile their altars high with offerings and with candles. Harken to me, Tethys, divinity of water, and help me, a sea-god.

Te. I have no power above the water, as I used to have, for this nymph has received from my own hand the sovereign power above the waves.
— Cho. This nymph has received...

Gl. And who is this nymph? Is it a Nereid?

Te. No, for the sea has given birth to no nymph.

Gl. I know — it is Venus.

Te. You are still wrong. She has driven Venus back to the gardens of Cnidos.

Gl. Then it is Juno.

Te. You are wrong.

Gl. Is it the French Juno?

Te. It is not Juno, it is Louise, and her name has more power than all the names of Juno.

* * *

When the dialogue came to an end, the fountain passed before their Majesties and went slowly back, and during its progress the music, as described before, began again and continued until the fountain went behind Circe's garden, leaving the hall empty.

When it was behind the castle the nymphs descended from the fountain and immediately entered the hall through the two trellises. Ten violin players, five on each side, dressed in white satin enriched with pure gold, plumed and decorated with egret feathers, began to play the first entrance of the ballet. After the violins there entered twelve pages, through the same arbors, six on each side. When they had all taken their places, quickly following them came twelve Naiads, six through one arbor and six through the other. No sooner were they seen by the violins than they [the violins] changed rhythm, to start the second part of the ballet, when the nymphs moved dancing up to the King and the Queen Mother, in the following pattern. At the first passage of the entrée there were six abreast in one line across the hall and three in front in a broad triangle, of which the Queen marked the apex, and three others behind her did the same. Then, as the music changed, they also moved in and out among each other, now in one direction, now in another, and then returned to their first position. When they had reached a place near the King, they continued the ballet, now composed of twelve geometrical figures, each different. During the last passage the violins played a very gay tune called "La Clochette".

Music for the first ballet, à 5. (p. 56)

Circe, still hidden in her garden behind closed curtains, no sooner heard the music of "La Clochette" than she emerged, very angry, holding her golden wand high in her hand. She came forward the whole length of the hall, to where the nymphs stood (arranged in a crescent facing their Majesties); she touched them one after another with her golden wand, and at her touch each became motionless as a statue. She did the same to the musicians, who could no longer play or sing, but stood motionless. Then Circe returned to her garden with as bold and joyous an expression as has a captain who has achieved a victory in some perilous and difficult enterprise.

LA PREMIÈRE ENTRÉE

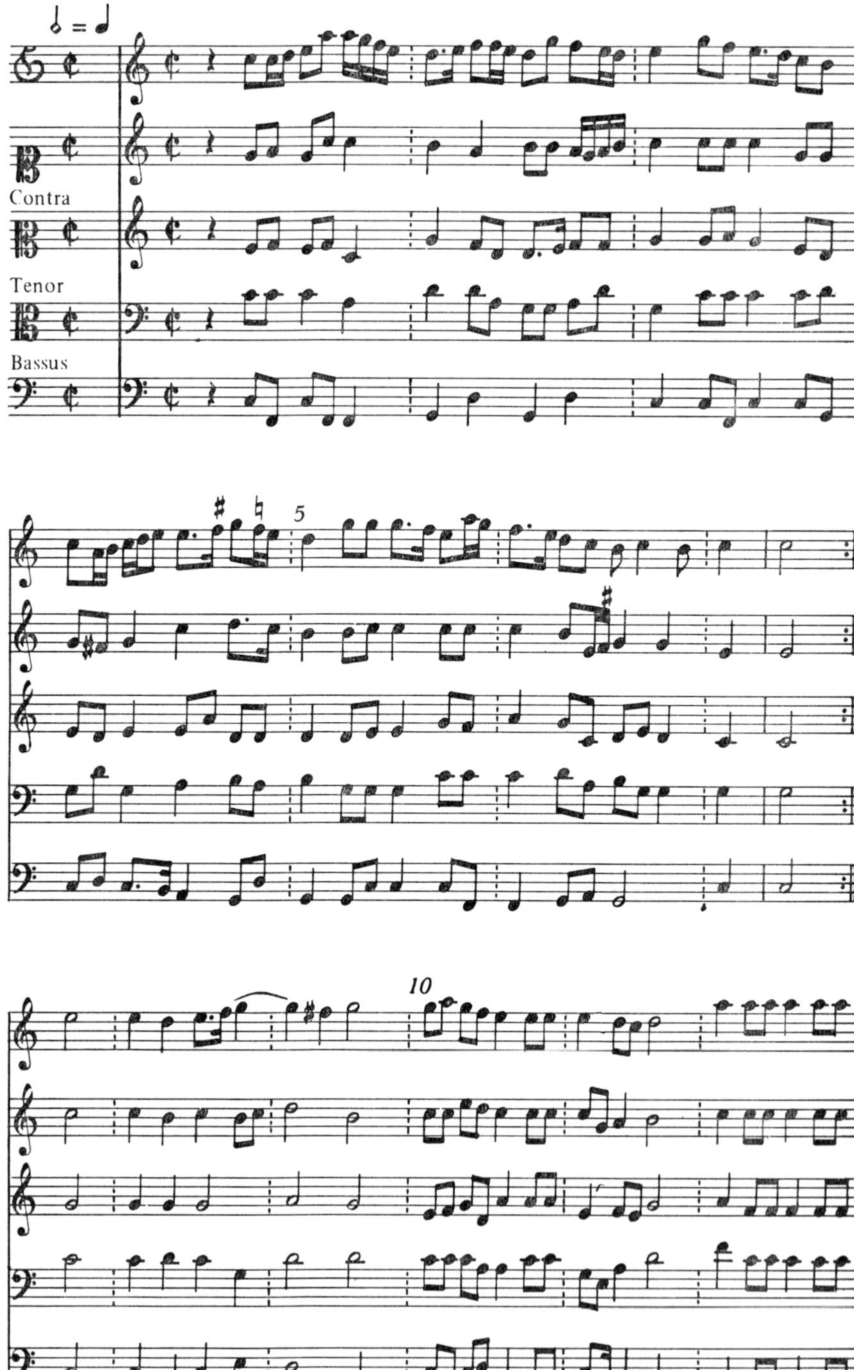

15
20
25

1) notated 

She was right to rejoice after having overcome such great courage as the nymphs had shown.

When Circe had retired to her garden in such glory — Lo! from the very highest part of the hall above the cloud, there came a great clap of thunder, which reverberated for some time. When it had ceased, the cloud which we have described began to descend slowly. Enveloped in it was Mercury, Messenger of Jupiter, sent by him to earth to break the enchantment of Circe with a piece of the Moly root. Mercury was clad as the poets describe him, in Spanish red satin embroidered carefully with gold. His shoes were gilded, with wings at the heels, signifying the swiftness of his running. His head was covered with a small winged gilded cap, his mantle was of violet cloth of gold. In his hand he carried the caduceus with which he had put Argus to sleep to accomodate Jupiter. This god, as he descended, sang tunefully the following song. He was represented by the Sieur du Pont, a gentleman of the King, a man of many accomplishments.

Mercury's Song (Music, p. 60)

I am the messenger of all the Gods,
with winged feet, clever and swift.
With the caduceus I go to the deep abyss
to ravish spirits from the Fates, to make them
live again. When they have been reborn I cast them down again.

I have taught men to obey the law, the sciences
and the arts and the cities are mine, and together
with wealth, I give eloquence. To cure a mind deprived
of its reason which, when it is tired of virtue, has been
charmed by pleasure, I bring the powerful root of the Moly.

By means of it I prevented Ulysses, who reached the shores of Italy, from becoming a pig, when he was enchanted by the arts of the sorceress Circe. In a castle she had built in France, she converted many a man into an animal, and not long ago charmed the water-nymphs.

This Circe has a shameless look in her eyes which at their first glance makes every man uncertain, and Cupid has no more effective dart. But past pleasure becomes odious to her, makes her ashamed; she makes men forget themselves, and together with their reason they lose their human form.

She knows how to bend the nymphs to her will, but she cannot convert them into monsters, for their godly nature makes them unchangeable. She makes the gods afraid of her, striking them with her golden wand, making them stand more solid than rock.

CHANSON DE MERCURE

I intend to expose the illusions of her art. I have had Moly distilled into a water of forgetfulness, and by my stronger powers I will undo hers. I know how much power and vigor she possesses, but great danger passed is a pleasure to the victor, who is honored by the name of a powerful adversary.

While Mercury was still in the air about two feet above the heads of the nymphs, when he had ended the song, he sprinkled the juice of the Moly root, which he had in a golden flask, over the heads of the nymphs. He sprinkled it around so effectively that it fell also on the musicians. No sooner were they wet by this water than they began to play again, the nymphs also started to dance and continued their ballet just as before they were enchanted. Now Circe, thinking that Mercury was doing her a great wrong by attacking her art, resolved to make him feel what she could do, and the power she had over him and even over the power of his caduceus. With this purpose, suddenly issuing forth from her garden, she ran furiously to the middle of the room, passing through the troupe of dancers as she had done before. She touched them a second time and the musicians also, restoring them to the condition from which Mercury had rescued them, and stepping back four paces, she began the following speech.

CIRCE'S HARANGUE

Man is never able to live content with his lot, but always hopes for more good fortune, he never finishes his goals nor his labors. He even imagines himself bored with an age when people lived idly, doing no work, when Saturn, banished from Heaven, ruled the earth.

The wandering people, controlled by nature like the animals, fed itself on the fruit which the forest produced without cultivation, and for police and law had only its own customs. But Jupiter drove out this unproductive domestic idleness of men, and put cleverness in their dull mind, in order to sharpen it with care and with labor. And he caused them to divide up the earth, which had been fertile when it had belonged to everyone and now became sterile without the sharp plow, and would not open its bosom or nourish its mortal children with its fruits.

Then Necessity taught cultivation of the earth, and people acquired all the other arts by practice. Everyone wanted to benefit by the earnings of his trade, and by doing good put others under obligation to him. Then Ambition, inspired by pleasure, changed our first way of living into customs which are called "vices". For people call "virtues" the way of living of our ancestors, which is supposed to be better, just as if the changing seasons and centuries were not, as they change, each exactly like the other.

Every human action is the result of desire, to which one is mated or led by Pleasure. Pleasure is the guide to repose or to labor which controls the movement of the will, and the actions which are pleasing and which are done in unison become the rule of life and the law for all of us. But soon people begin to dislike the manners of the present time and the reputation of past centuries increases. For envy had no power against the dead, and a dead man is held to be a god. This is what makes us honor the memory of the men who lived in the Golden Age. The long span of years makes us admire it because of regret for the past and makes us desire it because of disdain for the present. So everyone is annoyed and would like to change his life, without, however, dying. Everyone would like to change his actions, some want idleness, incited by their own inclination; some desire, armed with tempest and war, to drench the earth's surface with blood; some, instead of living in caves carpeted with moss, would like to live in a panelled palace with a ceiling starred with glittering gold, effacing the flaming torches of the all-embracing sky.

I am the only cause of all this change, which occurs from rank to rank, from moment to moment. My father, ceaselessly moving and revolving, limits the end of one season with another. The Sun above makes the ages change. Destiny in this way links all things together. Sad mortals, neither by vows nor prayers can you prevail upon the Three Spinning Sisters to quicken or slow down their handiwork. In it they spin not only the fate of gods and men, but also the destiny of armies which fly on wings of good or evil fortune.

The water nymphs tried once to thwart Destiny and bring the Golden Age back to France, where already a great temple of marble had been erected to Justice. But I made them stand motionless, solider than a rock, which with its back extending from the river bank turns aside the waves; solider than Niobe who can be seen near the walls of Sipyle — Niobe, who weeps ceaselessly, who dared to rival Latona in good fortune.

I am going to imprison this frivolous Mercury who has come to help these Nymphs, presuming on his cleverness and and his courage. He expects to have some power against my golden wand, and spoil my plans with a root that served Ulysses once as a medecine against my poisons, but Pallas, who was protecting Ulysses and not he himself, saved him from my works. Alone among the Gods I fear this Minerva, she alone can protect men from my arts. Mercury, volatile, changeable and foolish, urged first one way then another by caprice, without decision and without counsel, Mercury alone is weak and without power, unless Pallas gives him advice and assurance. At present in his pride he has refused her help. He is so full of temerity, so vain and presumptuous, that not only can he not by any means aid the nymphs with Ulysses' Moly, but he himself will be charmed by my wand and I shall keep him vanquished and imprisoned in my tower.

* * *

When she had finished her speech she approached Mercury, who was still enveloped in the cloud. Raising her golden wand she smote him with it. No sooner did he feel the blow than, dropping his caduceus, he became enchanted and the cloud bore him motionless to earth. Taking him by the hand she led him to her garden, followed by the nymphs, walking in file two by two, with no movements except those which appeared given them by Circe's spell. When Circe had entered her garden, the nymphs disappeared suddenly, without anyone's being able to see what became of them. At this moment the curtain hiding Circe's garden fell, one could see clearly and openly the beauty of the delicious garden, shining with a thousand fires and lights.

In addition one could see Circe seated majestically at the gate of her castle, with the spoils of her victory, for Mercury was lying on his back at her feet. He could not move without the permission and command of the enchantress. After the opening of the curtain a great stag, coming from the garden, passed before Circe, followed by a dog, the dog by an elephant, the elephant by a lion, the lion by a tiger, the tiger by a pig, the pig by other animals pêle-mêle. All were men transformed in this guise by her magic and the power of her enchantment.

When the preceding act had ended, the second intermedio

began to enter through the other trellis. This intermedio was composed of eight Satyrs, seven of them playing flutes, only one singing. He was Lord Saint Laurens, the King's Chamber Singer. The sound of this music was pleasing to the King, Queens, Princes and Princesses, as well as to all those present, because it was new and full of great gaiety. The Satyrs, as they made the circuit of the hall, continued their playing and to each of the verses one of the bands in the vault answered, as you will see forthwith. (Pl. V)

The Satyrs' Song

Oh Pan, angry Diana has abandoned the forest, as have the
wood-nymphs who used to trample the grass dancing in time
with the sweet sounds of thcir voices.

Chorus: Joy and sorrow, fear, hope, despair, Follow every changing,
immutable Fate's decree.

On their ivory lyres they sang of the victory of Jupiter,
king of the gods, armed with thunder and storm. He brought
the madness of the Giants to his victorious feet.

Cho. Joy . . .

Their dance was delectable and their voices agreeable;
Phoebus also enjoyed it. When they sang of France, its laws,
its kings, it abundance, their verses pleased us even more.

Cho. Joy . . .

fo - rêts ab - sen - té - e, Et tant de nym-phes des
fo - rêts ab - sen - té - e, Et tant de nym-phes des
fo - rêts ab - sen - té - e, Et tant de nym-phes des
fo - rêts ab - sen - té - e, Et tant de nym-phes des
fo - rêts ab - sen - té - e, Et tant de nym-phes des bois
bois Qui sou- laient des - sous leur dan - ce Pres - ser l her - be à
bois Qui sou - laient des - sous leur dan - ce Pres - ser l'her-be à la
bois Qui sou - laient des - sous leur dan - ce Pres - ser l'her-be à la
bois Qui sou - laient des - sous leur dan - ce Pres - ser l'her - be à la
bois Qui sou - laient des - sous leur dan - ce Pres - ser l'her - be à
la ca - den - ce Des doux ac - cords de leur voix.
ca - den - ce Des doux ac - cords de leur voix.
ca - den - ce Des doux ac - cords de leur voix.
ca - den - ce Des doux ac - cords de leur voix.
la ca - den - ce Des doux ac - cords de leur voix.

LA RÉPONSE DE LA VOUTE DORÉE

The song which strikes our ears is marvellously pleasing when it celebrates the virtue of a King, most just, who by his demeanor, not by force, combats vice.

Cho. Joy . . .

* * *

When they reached the trellis from which they had started, they perceived before them a woodland, twelve feet in diameter, three feet high, constructed in the shape and form of a large round mound of earth. Around this flower-bed and mound, well-aligned and arranged in four rows, were fine leafy trees and in the middle of the mound a piece of rock emerged, upon which was a large tree whose branches interlaced and mingled with the branches of the other trees, making a thick and pleasant bower. The whole ground consisted of thick grass with flowers mingling in the greenery, in which one could see lizards and snakes crawling and, as it were, leaving tracks. The oaks in the grove were loaded with golden acorns reproducing the real ones to the life. The big tree was artistically contrived on top of the rock, where were seated four Dryads with their backs to the tree (Pl. VI). They were dressed in the antique manner in green gold cloth, all covered with bouquets of gold and Italian silk, which signified their power over growing things. The outer sleeves, of gold crêpe and silk, were very wide and turned back nearly to the shoulders. The inner sleeves were the same color as the dress. The decorations of their necks and arms represented foliage and the ornament on their heads was that which was attributed to nymphs, since they were circled with oak leaves and hawthorn in the form of garlands. Pearls and precious stones were not spared nor golden crêpe and silk, flying in all directions, which displayed the munificence of the person who was presenting this superb and excellent ballet. And just as when in ancient times it was believed that these nymphs dwelt in the forests and ruled there, in the same way they now had on their heads three bouquets of oak leaves and acorns, and in their arms chaplets and garlands of flowers, all of them made of gold and silk. Behind her left shoulder each wore suspended a bundle or quiver of burnished gold, full of arrows, and held a stringed bow in her hands. They had the bearing and the look of bold and chaste huntresses.

When the grove, thus occupied, appeared to the Satyrs, they immediately changed their tune and sang the following song, which lasted until they presented themselves before the King. The orchestra from the golden vault never failed in its duty and habit of answering with voices and instruments.

Second Song of the Satyrs (Music p. 69)

> These nymphs now come forth from the woods at our call, and immortal Diana no longer conceals herself because she is angry.
>
> With a belt of white leather she has trussed her skirt at her side, and has gone to hunt a wild stag in the forest.
>
> As she went she said, "Go, Nymphs, just as if you were following me. Go quickly, Dryads. Go wood nymphs, to pay honor to the Valois, whose royal grandeur equals that of the gods."

* * *

This troupe having approached their Majesties (the four nymphs played by Ladies de Victry, Surgères, Lavernay, and Estavay la jeune, all ladies-in-waiting to the Queen), Mlle de Victry alone rose and began to recite to the King the following verses, so clearly and with such modest assurance, that the connaisseurs present, who had not known about her up till this moment, came to the conclusion immediately that her liveliness of mind made her capable and worthy of higher and more difficult things in the sciences and disciplines.

LE SECOND CHANT DES SATYRES

THE DRYADS TO THE KING

This green branch, which spreads its serrated leaves as a crown, and the acorn which hangs over our foreheads, show clearly that we are goddesses, living in the forest, guests of the ancient oaks. Our minds are free from evil, we who, with a body formed of air, are half-man and half-god. Great Jupiter the sole wielder of the thunderbolt, who moves the heavens and arrests the earth, ever quiet, ever the same, he who created matter and proclaims the laws of Destiny, [is] the artisan of All, the perpetual order of which Fate disposes.

Nevertheless we are subject to actions, subject to change and to other passions, because of the fear which mortal men feel of hate and of desire; the senses are moved by them as well as the understanding changed by thoughts. Our labor however is suited to our high rank, our work is divine, whereas man busies himself with his private affairs or with affairs of State.

But the mind which on its own responsibility tries to follow virtue is often combatted by a false image of good which, without any corruption of form or content, gives way to vice and loses its original purity. They are those people who are said to have been charmed by deceit, whom the witches have emprisoned in a pen by spells and by the blood of inhuman sacrifice, in order to have them ready for their crimes, attracted by the hope of vain honor. What can one expect from a wretched human being? Nothing but a vain thing! So Circe transforms men into a malformed creature, a tiger, an elephant, a great stag or a bear, forever deformed unless they have help.

The Water goddesses, bewitched by her wand, are standing before her castle, without movement, without breathing nor voice, motionless as logs. Mercury also let himself be overcome and captured — he who tried to defend the Naiads against Circe. Anyone who deceives himself with vain hope, who fears and for his conduct accepts any other advice except that of his original innocence, is easily vanquished by the sorcerer's arts. She seduces him in her pleasure-castle and seals the eyes of his mind with darkness.

Never has this passion of hope or of fear entered the heart's virtue of these nymphs; hope which arouses vanity, as fear engenders cowardice, assailing those who are not content with what true nature has given them.

I am the nymph Opis who places the arrows in Diana's quiver, who follows her in the forest and leads her troupe of huntresses. They are enemies of Love, of Games and of Idleness. We are going, all together, to ask Pan to come with us to the aid of the nymphs.

The lady having finished her speech, the wood came before the King, then moved slowly toward the thicket of Pan. Immediately the curtain hiding the thicket fell, presenting to the spectators the marvelous beauty of the scene. All the trees of the grove were loaded with lighted lamps and scattered around these were a hundred flaming tapers, which made the shady spot as bright and clear as daylight. In the middle was the god Pan, seated on a grassy spot before the cave which I have described to you before. Pan was played by Lord Juvigny, the King's equerry, and a gentleman favored by the Muses and Mars. When he saw the wood nymphs approaching his temple, he began, to show his pleasure at their coming, to play upon his pipes, which in early times he had invented. Then one heard sweet, pleasant and harmonious music from the organs in the cave behind Pan. When the soft music from the organs had ceased, Mlle. de Victry spoke to the god Pan as follows:

Opis, the Dryad, to Pan

O Pan — you who keep your Satyrs firmly in control, and manage all the elements in an eternal band; you who change everything without changing your own nature, giving nourishment to all things, all the time; you who are able to arrange everything in the universe, whom none of the gods dare oppose; guardian of the nymphs — now is not the time to take your pleasure playing your flute in this solitary grove. It is not Jupiter, nor is it Neptune; it is not one of the giants, hardened by combat; it is not dark, bold Pluto, King of the damned, who has command over Rage, over Cerberus, over Death, over a hundred different monsters, who opened the depths of his Hell. It is — and alas! shame closes my lips upon the words! — it is an enchantress, Circe, filled with pride, sorrow and scorn, who, in this castle which you see nearby, holds as prisoners not only some water nymphs but she secretly brought Mercury there, where she keeps men transformed into animals locked up in her park.

It is torture to be a slave, but this servitude of one who does not deserve it is still more rude and rough. Pan, master and King of All, do not allow Circe to defeat and conquer you. Already she is gloating enough over her trophies, since she is keeping your fairies in her castle — she who, by the sound of her voice alone can empty the waters of Naiads and the woods of Dryads.

When she had finished speaking, Pan rose and answered the Dryads in these words.

Pan's Answer

Be silent, sweet Opis, and you, gay Satyr, cease sounding your musette and go tell the others playing in the woods to assemble here, on my orders. And you, sister Dryads, divine troupe of the forest, do not turn pale because of the fear which troubles your breasts. Be certain of me, nymphs, be certain that Circe will feel the fire of my anger.

Immediately the Dryads came down from their grove and took their places in the four niches which were around Pan, all facing the room; next, the Satyrs also entered the wood, lying on the grass around Pan. They began once again the song they had sung at their entrance, and the musicians in the golden vault answered each couplet. During the song the Dryads' wood retired and left the hall.

When this woodsy music had ceased, another troupe issued from the other trellis, constituting the third intermedio. It was composed of the four Virtues, acted by four maidens dressed in sky blue, their dresses decorated with stars of burnished gold, symbolizing the perfection of those who accompany and follow Virtue. (Plate VII).

Their coiffures were horse-shoe shaped, of gold and silk, and above their heads were seen three large shining stars. The first bore a column, the second scales, the third a serpent, and the fourth an urn. Two of them were playing lutes and the two others were singing. They gave great pleasure to the audience with the sweetness of their lovely voices. They sang the following song and the golden vault answered them.

Song of the Virtues (Music p. 74)

Oh Gods, whose daughters we are, Gods, protectors of men,
come down from Heaven with us; powerful Gods, follow the lead
of the Virtues, your kinswomen, to France which you guard.

Men call me Prudence, sure defender of the mind, which
foresees events by my influence. When I descended from Heaven
I made myself guardian of the mind of this great King.

I, moderate Temperance, queen of the Golden Age, at his birth I suckled him. He transformed my milk into his own being as it fed him, and took control over pleasure.

And I have impressed in his breast a wise disdain of fear, from the time my hand rocked his cradle. So, with striking prowess, from his earliest youth he has amassed green laurels of victory.

He has praise for the Right and punishment for the Wrong in his scales of Justice. Because of him France is now my dwelling place, the place of Justice, the honored temple of the Law.

He is at this moment arming his stern hand against the base sorceress, who charms people's eyes. Descend, Oh Pallas! and do not disdain to be the companion of this virtuous Prince.

When the Virtues had passed before the King, the Queen Mother and the Princes, and had made the tour of the hall, as the others had done, there appeared through the same arbor through which they had entered, a very beautiful, rich and magnificent chariot drawn by a great serpent. The chariot was four feet high in front, eight feet in the middle, and eighteen in the rear. It was lined and decorated all around with coats of arms, with books and musical instruments, all in relief, of gold and burnished silver. And among the sheaves and coats of arms one could perceive a goodly number of faces and masques, lending grace to the whole structure. In the rear, at the highest point of this triumphal chariot, was Mlle de Chaumont, representing the goddess Minerva, dressed in cloth of gold, her corselet of cloth of silver, in the middle of which, both

CHANT DES QUATRE VERTUS

RÉPONSE DE LA VOUTE DORÉE AUX VERTUS:

à chaque couplet c'était une musique de douze instruments sans voix.

front and back, was depicted the frightful face of Medusa, of burnished gold. Her helmet and decorations of her head were of silver cloth, enriched with an infinity of stones and pearls of inestimable worth. At the back of the helmet was a *panache* made of egret plumes. The goddess bore in her right hand her gilded lance and in her left the shield and pavis, on which was painted the head of Medusa, of burnished gold and silver. Around the chariot were a hundred wax tapers which lighted up the equipage in a marvellous way. But it was even more illuminated by the grace and dignity of Mlle de Chaumont, who in no way was deficient in the majesty which is attributed to Minerva. Nature herself seemed to have endowed this lady with these treasures. (Plate VIII).

The four Virtues, seeing Pallas coming, immediately placed themselves beside the chariot, two on each side. The chariot, drawn by the serpent, advanced to the steps where the king was seated. Meanwhile, the band in the gilded vault, composed of instruments and voices both, began as follows, so sweetly and harmoniously, that the astonished audience thought they heard, at the arrival of the goddess, a part of Heaven's celestial harmony.

Song (Music p. 77)

Virtue dwells eternally in the soul,
Everything else must soon perish;
Meanwhile vice combats the virtues.
Nature made her laws unchanging,
The elements become stable through discord;
Even love is born from strife.

When the chariot had arrived before the King and the music had ended, Pallas, rising to her feet, addressing the King in a grave, loud and easily understood voice, spoke as follows:

MINERVA TO THE KING

I sprang completely armed from the head of Jupiter, when it had been split with an axe; the great God gave birth to me from his divine brain, and he himself carried me in his arms to the highest part of starry Olympus, where I was suckled. He left Mercury as my companion.

Sup.
Sup. II
Contra
Tenor
Tenor II
Bassus
Ver - tu en l'âme im-mor - tel - le de - meu - re, Il faut qu'en bref toute au - tre cho - se meu - re, Pour -

tant le vice aux ver - tus se com - bat: Na-ture se fit ses
tant le vice aux ver - tus se com - bat: Na - ture se fit ses
tant le vice aux ver - tus se com - bat: Na - ture se fit ses
tant le vice aux ver - tus se com - bat: Na - ture se fit ses
tant le vice aux ver - tus se com - bat: Na - ture se fit ses
tant le vice aux ver - tus se com - bat: Na - ture se fit ses
lois ir - re- vo - ca - bles, Par le di - scord les é - lé-ments sont
lois ir - re - vo - ca - bles, Par le di - scord les é - lé-ments sont
lois ir - re - vo - ca - bles, Par le di - scord les é - lé-ments sont
lois ir - re - vo - ca - bles, Par le di - scord les é - lé-ments sont
lois ir - re - vo - ca - bles, Par le di - scord les é - lé-ments sont
lois ir - re - vo - ca - bles Par le di - scord les é - lé - ments sont

I received rare gifts from his hand: Reason, which controls the gentle human mind; and he granted me control over quick thoughts, and with it I preside over men's understanding. To Mercury, in like manner, he granted the Senses, winged brothers lighter than air, changeable as it is, and flighty, which shift now here, now there; the desire for courage, leading the will by imagination, at one time to virtue, at another time to idle pleasure.

Those who arrive laboriously at virtue always have my support; others without me have followed pleasure, their thoughts always ravished by hope and fear, always without a guide following a deceitful path, they are drowned in the deep gulf of pleasure. But they do not die, for the soul never dies. He who dies a living death lives in sin, lacking judgment, in the fearsome shackles of lust which charm the mind without reason — such are those whom Circe leads to her palace and whom she conquers with vain thoughts.

Now Mercury, seeing these simple nymphs who had vanished along Circe's path, Mercury boldly came down from Heaven without me in order to change their enchanted bodies. Now he himself, deceived as to his vain prudence, perceives that without Reason, eloquence and the sweet speech which is his weapon is worth very little, because he himself has remained enchanted in her palace.

Great King, descendant of the Gods, of the race of Dardanus, upon whose head the flowers of Heaven are entwined, whose golden sceptre has come from the stars, a sceptre which Jupiter held in his hands, Circe alone remains to be combatted in France. Other similar castles you have had me destroy. I have heard you call me; I go to serve you and to ravish from Circe her castles, her spells, her lands.

Having ended her speech, when her chariot had made a turn around the hall and stopped in the middle of it, with sad and proud countenance she raised her eyes toward the sky and invoked Jupiter in these words.

MINERVA TO JUPITER

Oh my father, who are bathed in the wave of the golden cloud, from which I perceive you regarding mortal men, Oh, Father, descend! Oh Father, cause the cloud to open and reveal your face flaming with lightnings. I know that, certain of victory, I could alone enter this combat without calling on you. I am armed with a shield of seven layers of steel, covered with the poisonous hide of Medusa, with her hair of serpents. Her fatal look poisons and penetrates this metal, which turns into hard stone the body of any person who sees it, without changing his appearance. This fate is shared by gods and men, and you, Jupiter, are lawgiver to all the world. For he who has no real part in a quarrel deserves to be rebelled against later, even if he has won, and his enemies have made submission to him on bended knee. You have single-handed assumed the defence of the world and anyone who tried to help you, presumptuous in his pride, would commit a grievous offense, as if you were not powerful enough to defend it.

You well know (for the night conceals nothing from your eyes) that Circe has never ceased to do evil, envenomed by the horror of her spells. For my sake, thunder from on high with your blazing arrows, take in your hand a thunderbolt like a black cloud, and ravage the very foundations of this infamous place.

After this prayer, one heard from above the clouds a great noise and clap of thunder, which continued for a long time. When it stopped one could see the cloud descending, little by little, so that it seemed like a cloud of smoke, so cleverly was the illusion maintained. And during the descent the musicians of the golden vault began to sing with new instruments, different from the previous ones. It was the most learned and excellent music that had ever up till that time been played and heard, as will be seen from the following piece.

* * * *

O fortunate is heaven, which with its new stars Jealously effaces all other stars.
O fortunate also the land under these Princes.
Fortunate also the ship of France, lighted by its stars: Fortunate their laws, which will banish vices and war.

* * * *

When the music ended Lord Savornin (who is in the service of the King and is endowed with many fine talents, being principally a very fine singer and composer of music), representing Jupiter, appeared in the cloud. He was clad in a suit of cloth of gold; his

The Music which was performed in the golden vault during Jupiter's descent. There were forty musicians, voices and instruments both.

5
Ja - loux ef - fa - ce - ra tous les au - tres flam - beaux,
Ja - loux ef - fa - ce - ra tous les au - tres flam - beaux,
Ja - loux ef - fa - ce - ra tous les au - tres flam - beaux,
Ja - loux ef - fa - ce - ra tous les au - tres flam - beaux,
Ja - loux ef - fa - ce - ra tous les au - tres flam - beaux,
Ja - loux ef - fa - ce - ra tous les au - tres flam - beaux,
10
O bien heu - reux en - cor sous ces prin - ces la ter -
O bien heu - reux en - cor sous ces prin - ces la ter -
O bien heu - - reux en - cor sous ces prin - ces la ter -
O bien heu - reux en - cor sous ces prin - ces la ter -
O bien heu - reux en - cor sous ces prin - ces la ter -
O bien heu - reux en - cor sous ces prin - ces la ter -

15
- re, O bien-heu - reux aus - si le na - vi - re
- re, O bien-heu - reux aus - si le na - vi - re Fran -
- re, O bien-heu - reux aus - si le na - vi - re
re, O bien-heu - reux aus - si le na - vi - re Fran -
- re. O bien-heu - reux aus - si le na - vi - re
- re, O bien-heu - reux aus - si le na - vi - re

20
Fran - çais E - clai - ré de ses feux, bien heu - reu - ses leurs
- çais E - clai - ré de ses feux, bien heu - reu - ses leurs
Fran - çais E - clai - ré de ses feux, bien heu - reu - ses leurs
- çais E - clai - ré de ses feux, bien heu - reu - ses leurs
Fran - çais E - clai - ré de ses feux, bien heu - reu - ses leurs
Fran çais E - clai - ré de ses feux, bien heu - reu - ses leurs

25
loix, Qui ba - ni - ront d'i - ci les vi - ces et la
loix, Qui ba - ni - ront d'i - ci les vi - ces et
loix, Qui ba - ni - ront d'i - ci les vi - ces et
loix, Qui ba - ni - ront d'i - ci les vi - ces, les vi - ces
loix, Qui ba - ni - ront d'i - ci les vi - - ces
loix, Qui ba - ni - ront d'i - ci les vi - ces et

30
guer - - - re, Qui ba - ni - ront d'i - ci les
la guer - re, Qui ba - ni - ront d'i - ci les
la guer - - re, Qui ba - ni - ront d'i -
et la guer - re, Qui ba - ni - ront d'i - ci les
et la guer - re, Qui ba - ni - ront d'i - ci les
la guer - - re, Qui ba - ni - ront d'i - ci les

boots were of gilded leather and his cloak of yellow satin, trimmed with gold fringes, lined with golden camlet. He bore in one hand his sceptre, in the other the frightful thunderbolt, and on his head a fine crown, all made of burnished gold. Across his body he wore a rich scarf shining like the sun, because of the pearls and jewels that covered it. Between his legs was a great eagle of burnished gold. While he was still in the cloud he sang these verses.

CHANT DE JUPITER

Jupiter's Song

To help you I come down from Heaven, I am anxious about the world, oh Pallas! With watchful eye I watch over everything, over the gods in the sky, over mortals living restlessly, over Hades under the care of Pluto.

Nothing which has a living body and feelings, subject to many changes, remains in a permanent state. The connections grow corrupt and come unbound, and then later, without dying, are remade and take on from me a better existence.

Many mortal men enchanted into monsters, nymphs and gods whom Circe has conquered, will take on a more beautiful shape when they recover their reason. They need fear no more a sordid prison, harsh bonds, nor being enchanted again.

Dear Pallas, my daughter, look at me! Remain here, you are sister of this King, this King my son, flower of France's sceptre. Change his enemies with Medusa's stare and make his people humbly obedient under his just rule.

When the cloud had borne Jupiter to the ground, it rose again, and Pallas dismounted from her car, which in a moment left the room. Jupiter and she on foot joined the company in the grove of the god Pan. He, rejoicing at their arrival, began to play his seven-pipe flageolet, and the soft organs performed some new music. When this harmony came to an end, Minerva began to speak to Pan, as follows.

MINERVA TO THE GOD PAN

Pan, what good does it do you to have under your guard and in your power what heaven contains, since by carelessness you allow everything to be taken from you? That you allow and see Circe establish herself in the middle of your forest? The water nymphs who are under your care, she stopped with her spells when she surprised them in the road. She, a nymph in no way your equal, puts on all lips her great renown, oh unjust, cruel and ungrateful Pan, because she keeps Mercury in servitude.

This god, as a shepherd was taking his repose at the crest of Mount Cyllene, and was pasturing his flock of big sheep with horns and with golden wool on their backs, when he perceived the nymph Driope alone, her head covered with golden hair. He immediately fell in love with her. Driope conceived you by Mercury, your father.

And you, forever scorned by the Gods, disgrace to the heavenly race, can you allow the Gods to be insulted before your very eyes without helping? Can you permit a public disgrace, that a magician should hold your father prisoner? Often the opinion spread abroad by the common herd extends a fine reputation or destroys it completely. You have been thought by everyone to have fearful strength. If you want the honor of your name to be esteemed in the same way you must bring the same courage to the same deeds, and not let them diminish in power. The violent acts of ardent youth are not judged to be virtue nor prowess, they are the green flowerings of times to come, and they wither if time does not develop them into fruit.

PAN'S ANSWER TO MINERVA

Daughter of Jupiter, courageous Goddess, your own virtue makes you disdainful of others. Do not reproach me. I did not hide when the Giants tried to invade the Heavens. My reputation always animates me with courage. But he who runs a risk in vain is thought to be ill-advised. I saw Circe stop the nymphs and carry away Mercury; I would have run to their defense in vain. One must not resist the Fates. No one but you (for I know Destiny) can bring an end to Circe's art and her spell.

Then he came out of the wood followed by his eight Satyrs, each of whom bore a thick, knotty and spiny club. This group came forward to the middle of the room in the direction of the King, and after making deep and humble obeisance to him, began to make its way slowly toward Circe's garden. After them walked Minerva with two of the four Virtues on either side of her, and then Jupiter, alone, with the four Dryads in a line behind him. Thus the company presented the appearance of a battalion and troop of soldiers coming to attack and raze Circe's garden. Circe, seeing them, immediately suspected their plan and decided to oppose them valiantly. Since the assailants were about to attack the gate, she raised her golden wand in one hand and with the other she rang a bell in a tower of her castle. She had no sooner sounded the bell, when, from within, one could hear such a strange noise — baying, roaring, made by dogs, wolves, bears, lions, and an infinite variety of other animals — that the castle seemed about to break up and fall in ruins, or to fall upon the heads of the attackers. When this furious noise had somewhat abated, the enchantress, advancing boldly to the gate of her garden, raised her voice so loud that everyone could hear her, to accuse the Gods and Goddesses of making trouble, in the following verses.

CIRCE

Do you see them coming, all gathered together for this deed, do you see those Beings who dwell in the sky, in the golden stars, and who arm their hands with criminal flames, Oh Circe, immortal nymph, do you see them coming against you?

No! No! I have not, in fear, armed my breast with a shield where the head of Medusa suddenly transforms the enemy into stone. I would not wish it, for it is a reproach, which defames the name of the person who goes into combat with an unfair advantage. If I wish to attack, or if someone insults me, I seek my defence in myself alone.

That God with the golden chariot whose forehead shines, crowned with golden rays, who leads the dance of the fixed stars in an orderly fashion, who causes the years to pass with their changeable seasons, who lights the whole Heavens with his flame, and can consume the fires of Jupiter; that all powerful Sun, whom all Nature worships, who moves the Universe, my Father the Sun, giving soul and strength to all living things — that God does not allow me to freeze with fear in my heart.

So I can alter the course of great rivers, and make them smite the rocks of their sources with their foaming crests. The Moon has many times plunged into this forest, blackening the midnight hours when I gave the command, its face colored with shame, pale with fear.

If I please, I can resist you. Tell me, Jupiter, who it was that changed you so many times, into an eagle, or a bull, a satyr, or a swan? Admit it, oh conqueror, that there is no star or constellation shining in the warm sky, whose body I have not changed into a star.

I will resist you. If Destiny brings to an end the power of my golden wand, it is not in your favor, Jupiter. Do not believe it. If someone is soon to triumph over me, it is this King of the French. You must yield to him, as I am doing, the heavens which you possess.

This proud and arrogant speech irritated the company still more against her, so much that the god Pan, followed by his Satyrs, in anger began to assail furiously the gate of the garden, prison of the Naiads. Jupiter, his face bearing an expression of anger and annoyance, with his sceptre in one hand and his thunderbolt in the other, with bitter words, threatened to treat Circe as he had treated her brother Phaeton. To frighten her still more, the Dryads pretended to draw their bows at her. Nonetheless Circe, without being frightened by the threats of Jupiter and the nymphs, nor the actions of Pan, continued defending the entrance to the garden with her magic wand. The wand little by little lost its power under the influence of Minerva. She, when she had forced the gate, passed through the garden, followed by Jupiter after he had first smitten Circe with his thunderbolt so that she fell to earth as if deprived of all feeling. Jupiter had pity on her and raised her to her feet. But Pallas, not willing to lose the fruits of victory, went immediately to take possession of the wand by whose power so many marvellous things had been executed and brought to a conclusion. And to make her victory the more glorious and worthy of honor, taking Circe by the hand, she conducted her out of the garden and led her slowly the full length of the hall, accompanied by the four Virtues and followed by Jupiter, who was leading Mercury, now freed from enchantment. They were followed by the god Pan, accompanied by his Satyrs, and by the Dryads, who came last of all.

Minerva, having entered the presence of the King, presented him with the golden wand and with Circe, who, as if vanquished and deprived of her power, came to sit below the place where the Princes were. Then Jupiter presented to the King his two children, Mercury and Minerva, who cast themselves at the feet of his Majesty, giving to understand that they yielded to this great King in the power to command, in wisdom to govern, in eloquence to attract men, even those most far removed from the Right. All these virtues and powers the King had acquired from the wise counsels, instruction and conduct of the Queen Mother. She is much greater than all the princesses who were ever crowned, because she is the mother of such a great King, who is not accustomed to hide the great obligations, both general and particular, which he owes to her.

On the other hand, Pallas has yielded the honors for modesty, industry, and regal gravity to the Queen, wife of France's Jupiter, for seconding the virtues of her husband and for being (as she is) one of the most praised and admired princesses on earth.

After the defeat of Circe, the four Dryads returned to their niches, Pan and the Satyrs re-entered the forest and the hall was empty.

Then, while the spectators were waiting in silence, expecting something rare remaining to end the ballet, the violins began to play a very beautiful *entrée*. Now the Dryads rose and left their niches, to present themselves in a row in the middle of the hall. Then, turning their backs to the King, they went dancing toward the garden as though they were certain of the delivrance of the Naiads, for whom Jupiter and Pallas had labored so hard against Circe, jealous for the happiness of such a fine and blessed company.

As the Dryads regarded the garden, lo! the Naiads, now free from enchantment, suddenly and unexpectedly appeared in the garden, as if they had fallen from the clouds or had just emerged from deep hiding places in the earth. They proceeded two by two to the middle of the room. In the front rank walked the Queen, holding by the hand the Princess of Lorraine, a real heir to the goodness, piety and sweetness of the late Mme. Claude de France, daughter and sister of our Kings, whose memory will be forever honored in this kingdom by all persons who profess virtue and honor.

The others followed, two by two, each in her place, and leaving the garden they faced the four Dryads, who joined them.

At this point the violins changed their tone, and began to play the *entrée* of the Grand Ballet. It was composed of fifteen figures, arranged in such a way that at the end of each figure all the ladies turned to face the King. When they had appeared before the King's Majesty, they danced the Grand Ballet with forty passages or geometric figures. These were all exact and well-planned in their shapes, sometimes square, sometimes round, in several diverse fashions; then in triangles accompanied by a small square, and other small figures. These figures were no sooner formed by the Naiads, dressed (as we have said) in white, than the four Dryads, dressed in green, arrived to change the shape, so that as one ended, the other began.

At the middle of the Ballet a chain was formed, composed of four interlacings, each different from the others, so that to watch them one would say that it was in battle array, so well was order kept, and so cleverly did everybody keep his place and his cadence. The spectators thought that Archimedes could not have understood geometric proportions any better than the princesses and the ladies observed in this Ballet.

And in order that everybody should know what a variety of music was necessary, some grave, some gay, some in triple time, some for a gentle and slow dance, I have written it down, so that nothing should be lacking or imperfect in the description of what occurred.

Dance Music

LA PETITE ENTRÉE

1) × misplaced in print

La grand' entrée

f 57v - 58

25
f 58v - 59
30

35
f 59v - 60
40

45
f 60v - 61
50
55

60
f 61v - 62
65

70
f 62v - 63
75
Fin
dal

The Ballet ended, the Naiads and the Dryads made deep obeisance to his Majesty. Now the Queen, approaching the King, her husband, took his hand and presented him with a large medal of gold, upon which was a dolphin swimming in the sea. Everyone took this as a certain prophecy of what God was soon to provide for the happiness of the Realm. Following the Queen's example, all the other Princesses, ladies and maidens went according to their rank and degree to choose a Prince, a Lord, or a Gentleman, as they pleased. To each of them they presented a medal with their symbols, all things of the sea, because the ladies were representing water nymphs, as you can see from what follows.

Mme. la Princess de Lorraine gave M. de Mercure the Siren.
Mme. de Mercure gave M. de Lorraine Neptune.
Mme. de Nevers gave M. de Nevers a sea horse.
Mme. de Guise gave M. de Genevois Arion.
Mme. d'Aumalle gave the Marquis de Chausson a whale.
Mme. de Joyeuse gave the Marquis de Pont a sea monster.
Mme. la Maréchale de Retz gave M. d'Aumalle a Triton.
Mme. de Larchant gave M. de Joyeuse a branch of coral.
Mme. du Pont gave M. de Bourdeille an oyster in the shell.
Mlle. de Bourdeille gave M. de Nevers a swordfish.
Mlle. de Cypierre gave M. de Luxembourg a shrimp.
These are the presents which the water nymphs gave. The four Dryads, wood nymphs, gave the following:
Mlle. de Victry gave to M. Le Bastard an owl.
Mlle. de Surgères gave the Comte de Saulx a squirrel.
Mlle. de Lavernay gave the Comte de Maulevrier a stag.
Mlle. de Stavery gave the Comte de Boucharge a boar.
Minerva gave the Queen Mother Apollo.
Circe gave M. le Cardinal de Bourbon a book.

In this order and arrangement they led the Princes out to dance the great Ball, and when this was ended they started the Branles and other dances customary in great feasts and celebrations.

At the end of this, their Majesties the King and Queen retired.

The night was already well advanced, since the Ballet Comique had lasted from ten o'clock in the evening till half-past three in the morning. The length had tired none of the spectators and the contentment of everyone was great, principally because they saw such a high, excellent, grave and sovereign lady do such honor to her subjects as to lower herself to take part in the ceremonies which had been performed to please her, and to show herself in public. They all knew that our Kings and Queens, ruling over a free people, treat them frankly and with kindness, freedom (*franchise*), understanding and courtesy.

* * *

Allegory of Circe
that Natalis Comes has taken from the commentaries of Greek poets.

Circe, daughter of the Sun and of Perseis, daughter of Ocean, was a magician, and used to transform men into divers animals. Ulysses was preserved from her spells, and she could not transform him as she had done his companions. Circe, which means "a composite", is daughter of the Sun, which is Heat, and of a daughter of the sea, which is Humidity. Circe, then, is the composite of the elements which can only result from the movement of the Sun, her father, who is Form, and of Perseis, her mother who is Matter.

The four nymphs, who served her and gathered the herbs for her potions, are the elements over which she has no power, because the corruption, generation and mutation of the elements is perpetual.

It is said that she changed men into monstrous and divers shapes, because the corruption of one thing is the generation of another thing formed from it, but not in the first shape.

Ulysses was preserved by the gods because the human soul is immortal and divine, the body perishable and earthly.

Another Allegory, by the Sieur de la Chesnaye

Since there are other more general fables which mean universal generation, one can reduce this story to a more limited allegory, namely, that Circe is the revolving of the year, following the revolution of the Sun; the nymphs are the roots, grasses, flowers, and seeds. Ulysses, the great traveller, is Time, which never stops, always continuing; his transformed companions mean the Past and the Present. In the year Ulysses lived with Circe, she conceived four children by him, Auson (called Romanus), Caliphon, Marsus, and Telegonus, who are the four seasons. When Ulysses returned to Ithaca he was slain by his son Telegonus with a fish bone. So when the Sun, father of the seasons, has returned to the last segment of Sagittarius, the year has come to an end at the beginning of the sign half-fish and half-ram.

The Moral Allegory

Circe is called daugther of the Sun and of Perseis, because desire and lust come to animals from heat and dampness. If this stimulation and this natural impulse incites us to voluptuousness, overcomes us, it urges us to those vices which make us resemble animals, that is to say, lechery, drunkenness, cruelty and certain other vices. But the man who is endowed with Reason is protected against these poisons.

Ulysses means that part of the soul capable of reasoning. Circe is man's nature. Ulysses' companions mean both the powers and the qualities of the soul which work with and are in agreement with the affections of the senses which no longer obey the Reason.

Another Allegory of Circe, according to the opinion of Lord Gordon, a Scotsman, chamberlain of the King

To understand the allegory of Circe it is necessary to consider that all allegory of poetical fictions in general is based on natural philosophy, or on morality, or on the supernatural and divine, or on a mixture of one and the other. The specific allegory of Circe, as it is described by Homer in Book X of his *Odyssey*, seems to refer partly to what is divine and partly to what is natural and moral. Circe, according to Homer, is a goddess and therefore immortal. She is daughter of the Sun and a sea nymph. The etymology of her name, which is Greek, comes from κιρνᾶν (*cirnan*), which means "to mix", and it is true that everything is created from a mixture of the Sun, which causes all warmth, and the sea, which is the source of all humidity. The name of her mother is Perseis, and comes from the Greek περᾶν, which means "passing beyond", which is very suitable to the Sea, which ebbs and flows in perpetual motion from the banks and coasts of the earth, and by this movement preserves itself from dirt and infection. So we will assume that Circe, engendered by the Sun and the Sea, shares the qualities of both. The Sun by nature is the efficient cause of everything here below, with the help of moisture proceeding from the water which is in the veins of the earth. This same Sun signifies allegorically the clearness and light of the Truth and that Divine Spark which illumines our souls. The sea by nature nourishes and produces that which maintains and excites pleasure. For this reason the poets have pretended that Venus arose from the sea, and called her "aphrodite". Allegorically this may be taken for sensual pleasure, which frequently brings men to ship-wreck.

From these considerations it seems not unreasonable to take Circe for that desire in general which rules and dominates all living things and is a mingling of the divine and the sensual. It has very different effects, leading some men to virtue, others to vice. This is in agreement with the fact that she is called "Queen" and has at her service and in servitude to her nymphs and animals. By the nymphs, who are partly divine, are meant the virtues, and by the brute animals, vice and sensuality. For desire spurs to virtue those who are prepared for it by divine help; on the contrary, desire makes those who are destitute of good intentions and training into servants and slaves of vice. Circe's dwelling is a magnificent palace in a delightful place, a beautiful building, gilded and shining, which means that desire cannot be aroused without the appearance of beauty, either true or false. The person of this goddess is described as being extraordinarily lovely, endowed with everything attractive, her voice sweet and clear. This represents what may arouse desire, either by sight or hearing — desire to love virtue or its contrary; for desire for some people is an instrument of salvation, for others the instrument of perdition or ruin. The practice and occupation of this Circe is to sing and to create immortal works like those made by the goddesses. Her singing signifies divine eloquence and discourses about the Truth, and her works signify the virtuous acts done by those people who are motivated by the desire for glory, good renown, and immortality.

The Naiads and the Dryads are nymphs of the water and the woods, that is to say, the good spirits scattered throughout the universe. They are the servants of this queen, who live with her in pleasure and liberty. They occupy themselves with collecting the most exquisite herbs and flowers of the earth to serve the purposes of their mistress. They stand for the virtue and knowledge through which the minds of men are prepared and disposed for good. On the other hand, Circe had in her palace lions, bears, and wolves which had lost their original nature and had become cute and fawning like lap-dogs. This represents for us that mere brute lust causes the most worthy persons to lose courage and power and become slaves of lust.

Circe with one drink converted men into beasts and with another remedy restored to them their real shape and human form. By this the poets, first inventors of all philosophy, meant to convey to us that desire when it is used for luxury and vice, makes us more brutish than the brutes themselves; but if it is by divine help imbued with precepts of virtue, it renders to men their true form and delivers them from the bestial servitude of vice and lust, as is generally said.

The companions of Ulysses in particular came to this queen's realm badly supplied and prepared for virtue, called by the Greeks προαίρεσις, the power of choice. When they first arrived they amused themselves with drinking and eating, that is with sensual pleasure. This teaches us that those who abandon themselves to pleasure and intoxicate themselves with sensual delights become dirty as pigs and remain prisoners and captives of vice. But Ulysses, who is the virtuous man, when he meets this desire, aided by divine help, and provided with the Moly, meaning reason and the divine spark in our souls, is not changed from his human form. So, because of his worth and virtuous courage, he is victorious over desire and forces Circe to restore his transformed companions to their true human form. This teaches us that divine help is the only, the unique way to restrain desire from pleasure and from the captivity and servitude of delights.

From this discourse upon the allegory of the fable of Circe one can perceive the idea and the example of virtue which the Queen, accompanied by the Princesses and ladies of the court, represented under the guise of the Naiads. They signified the immortal pleasures and delights — those which induce desire directed by virtue to be used and exercized in the performance of generous and valorous actions, and to teach everyone that one must not desire what is beautiful and shining on the outside, but should desire interior and much less apparent beauty. On the other hand, by means of the animals, prisoners in Circe's palace, we have attempted to demonstrate the wretched servitude of those who are led by the brutish desire of lust, which seduces men by the appearance of external beauty and which is in truth ruin and eternal perdition.

FINIS

Pl. I Figure de la Salle

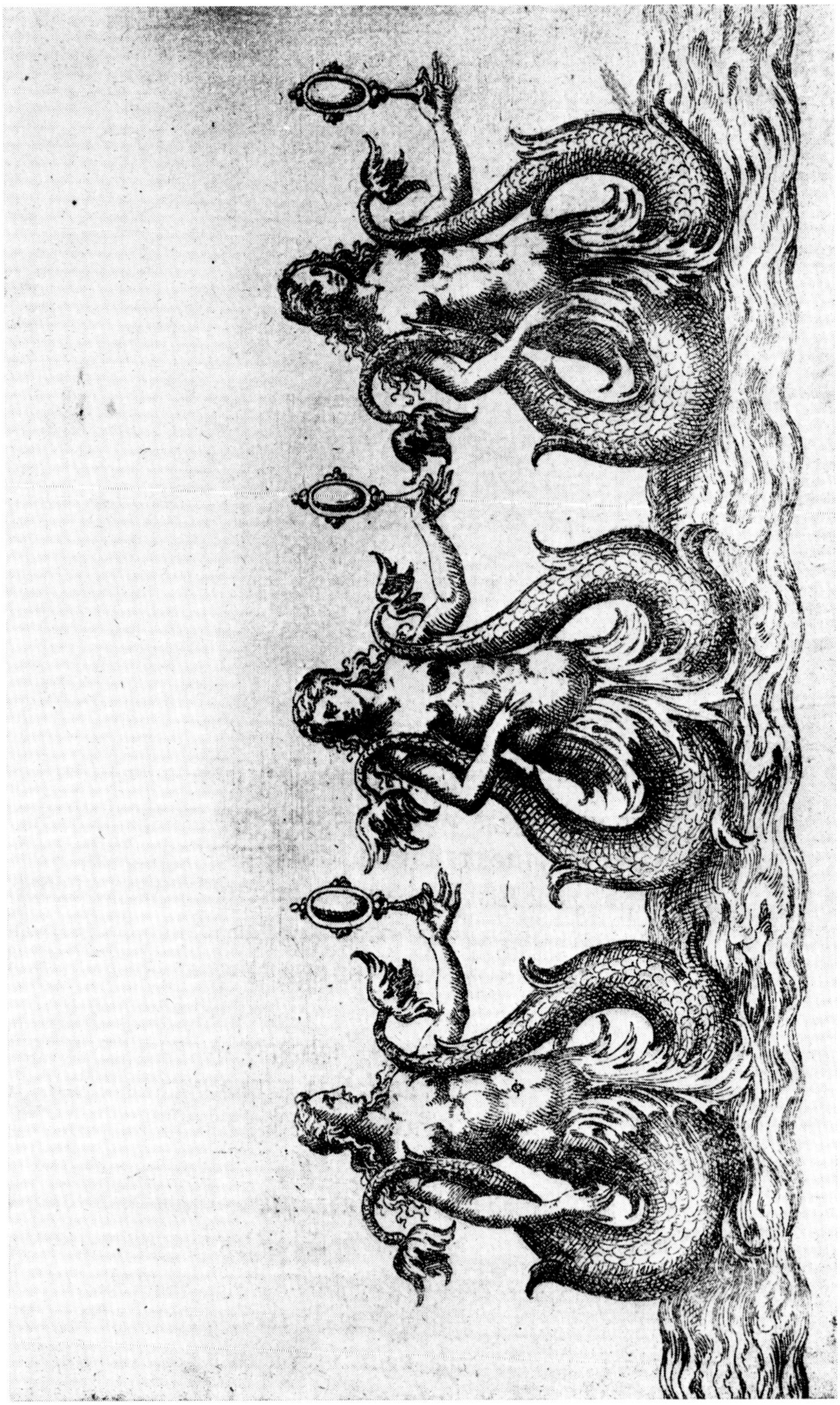

 Pl. II Figure des Sereines

Pl. III Figure de la Fontaine

Pl. IV Figure des Tritons

Pl. V Figure des Satyres

 Pl. VI Figure du chariot du bois

Pl. VII Figure des Quatre Vertus

 Pl. VIII Figure du chariot de Minerve